THE HARVEST

PREPARING THE LABORS FOR THE

END TIMES

Dr. Christine Renee

THE HARVEST

PREPARING THE LABORS FOR THE END TIMES

HAR Publishing, LLC
USA

The Harvest: Preparing the Labors for the End Times

By Dr. Christine Renee

Copyright © 2018 by Dr. Christine Renee

HAR Publishing, LLC
www.Harpublishing.com

Unattributed quotations are by Dr. Christine Renee. Unless otherwise stated,
all Scripture is taken from the King James Version (KJV) of the Bible.
First Edition 2018 Printed in the United States of America.

ISBN   978-0-9986296-1-2
Library of Congress Cataloging-in-Publication Data
LCCN: 2018911652

Contents

IX

This book is dedicated to all my colleagues in the gospel and fellow labors in ministry. And to all the people sitting in the pews just waiting to help reap the harvest.

Do you not say, there are yet four months and then comes the harvest? Behold, I say to you, lift-up your eyes and look on the fields, that they are white for harvest.

John 4:35

Preface

Get ready to embark upon a timely book loaded with information and techniques on how to win people into the kingdom of God. Soul winning is the heart beat of God and the lifeline of the local church. Throughout these pages, the author goes into details and practical applications on how to become an effective witness and soul winner for the Lord Jesus Christ. The author also lays out a strategic plan on how to train, equip, and how to send forth believers into the marketplace and *harvest fields,* to win souls and make disciples.

The methodologies and strategies presented in this book are meant to enhance any Christian's witness and evangelism skills. Whether its one-on-one evangelism, market place ministry, media ministry, para-church events, church gatherings, and or evangelistic meetings, etc... This book is essential and necessary to help get the message of the Lord Jesus Christ out to the masses and into the highways and bi-ways. This book will also help church leaders to prepare to gather the greatest harvest of souls ever to be won since church history.

Acknowledgements

I would like to acknowledge and thank all the many teachers, scholars, and spiritual mentors within the body of Christ. That have helped disciple and mentor me directly and indirectly throughout the years. Too many to name. If it were not for all the many teachings and instructions that I have received over the years. I don't think this book would have ever come about. I love God and I am forever grateful for Him sending His Son, Jesus Christ and Holy Spirit to redeem me and others from an eternal hell.

Jesus said to them, "follow Me, and I will make you fishers of men."

Matthew 4:19

I
Why Win Souls?

With the earth being over five billion years old, at the time of the writing of this book. And an estimate of over seven billion people living in the world. Only one-fourth of the population has ever heard the gospel preached. People who live in remote areas or in areas where the gospel is not allowed. May never hear the good news of the saving grace of the Lord Jesus Christ. This is why it is imperative that labors be made ready.

Soul winning is a mandate from the Lord Jesus Christ with specific strategies only the church can fulfil. In Mark 16:15, the Lord Jesus Christ commanded His disciples to go into the entire world to preach the gospel. With the Bible being the blue print the church must position itself and get ready to gather the greatest harvest of souls ever won since church history.

It is Gods will that none should perish. God wants all mankind to come into the saving revelation knowledge of who He is and who His son Jesus Christ is. (2 Peter 3:9). Therefore, it is imperative that God's kingdom be established in all the earth before the end of this dispensation of grace. It is up to the body of Christ. The body of believers to get all the necessary information and learn how to win souls at all cost.

God has always wanted a family. He has always wanted a kingdom of people that would bring Him glory and honor in the earth. Because of the finished works of the Lord Jesus Christ on Calvary. People can now be "born again" into the family of God, *interchangeably: the kingdom of God.*

The Bible teaches all have sinned and come short of the glory of God. We are all born into sin (*sinners*). However, Jesus Christ died in the place for all sin. Jesus was hung up on a cross for our hang-ups and when He died, He said, "It is finished". Meaning sin and eternal death has been defeated and the grave has lost its eternal power to hold all those who believe in Him.

Jesus became a sin sacrifice for the whole human race. He was put on the cross, crucified, died, and put in a grave, *tomb*. But after three days, He rose from the dead with all power and authority under His jurisdiction.

I Corinthians 15:55-56 states, oh death where is your victory and death where is your sting? For the sting of death is sin and the power of sin is the law. And the way to salvation is a right relationship with God the Father, through the shed blood of the Lord Jesus Christ. The gospel is the good news and the way to salvation and sanctification.

The resurrection of the Lord Jesus Christ is about how Jesus rose with all power over sin, death, and the grave. He also rose with power over sickness, diseases, bondages, and eternal damnation in hell. (Matthew 28:18). Therefore, no one should have to pay the price of spending their immortal soul in hell. Jesus paid the price for all sinners on the cross at Calvary. Salvation is the way into the kingdom of God. Jesus's victory over sin, death, and the grave gives every human-being, man, woman, boy, or girl the opportunity to be "born again". The "new birth" interchangeably with being "*born again*", gives every person access into the kingdom of God. And the church is the final product of Gods kingdom and plan for salvation.

Since, the way to salvation has been made through the death, burial, and resurrection of the Lord Jesus Christ. The question remains will all mankind come into the saving revelation knowledge of who Christ is? Will all be saved from eternal damnation, hell, and the wrath to come? The answer to these questions is *no*! Because not *every* person has heard, nor believed, or received Jesus Christ as their Lord and Savior.

Every person born into this earth doesn't come automatically knowing God's plan for salvation and redemption. And most importantly, most believers are *not* willing to go out into the highways and the bi-ways to tell of the saving grace of the Lord Jesus Christ.

There is a clarion call for all believers to go into the market place and be a witness and soul winner for the Lord Christ. Most Christians don't realize how important it is to be a witness. Therefore, many do not witness. This is an indictment on the church of the Lord Jesus Christ. The prophet Isaiah prophetically stated this is the reason why, hell has enlarged itself. (See Isaiah 5:13-14).

The wrath of God is real and hell is real. The Bible states that if anyone does not believe in the Lord Jesus Christ, on judgement day their spirit will be sentenced to live in hell with satan and demonic forces throughout eternity. They will be tormented day and night. Hell was never created for mankind. Hell was created for the devil and the fallen angels (See 2 Peter 2:4). In the book of Revelation 12:7-10, it states:

> [7]And war broke out in heaven. Michael and his angels fought with the dragon; and the dragon and his angels fought, [8] but they did not prevail, nor was a place found for them in heaven any longer. [9] So the great dragon was cast out, that serpent of old, called the Devil and Satan, who deceives the whole world; he was cast to the earth, and his angels were cast out with him.[10] Then I heard a loud voice saying in heaven, "Now salvation, and strength, and the kingdom of our God, and the power of His Christ have come, for the accuser of our brethren, who accused them before our God, day and night, has been cast down.

Note: God wants every human being to avoid going to hell by being presented the gospel of the kingdom of God. Which is the only way to salvation.

There is a biblical mandate for believers to go forth to all nations and cultures preaching the gospel of the kingdom with power and with love. Every believer will have to give an account to God for each and every day of their lives. (Romans 14:12). Therefore, we must begin to plant the seeds of God's Word into the hearts of those that do not believe. There is no better time than now to win souls. There's something each believer can do to influence others to receive Christ. Every unbelieving person at best should be given the opportunity to make Jesus Christ their Lord and Savior. Even if they reject the message of salvation, at least they have been given an opportunity to decide for themselves.

God never intended for mankind to go about life not knowing His Son nor the One who created them. Nor for anyone to spend eternity in torment. Soul winning for the Christian should be as natural as the daily work they do. Soul winning should not be a struggle nor grievous toil. Soul winning should be easy, delightful for the Christian and practiced daily.

Obedience is another reason why believers must win souls. Obedience helps bring about Gods plan of salvation and redemption in the earth. The Lord Jesus Christ wants us to win souls. Not only win them but make disciples (see Matthew 28: 18-20). Those who have had the privilege of coming into the kingdom of God must realize that soul winning is the heartbeat of God.

The believer must also be equipped to have a global mindset as far as preaching the gospel is concerned. Other nations and religions like Islam,

Buddhism, Hinduism, etc. are growing rapidly in their doctrine's, while the church continues to sleep right through the greatest harvest of souls in the history of mankind. It is imperative that the body of Christ, in these last days be prepared and made ready like the church in the book of Acts was. Acts 2:41-47 states:

> 41 Those who accepted his message were baptized, and about three thousand were added to their number that day. 42 They devoted themselves to the apostles teaching and to fellowship, to the breaking of bread and to prayer. 43 Everyone was filled with awe at the many wonders and signs performed by the apostles. 44 All the believers were together and had everything in common. 45 They sold property and possessions to give to anyone who had need. 46 Every day they continued to meet together in the temple courts. They broke bread in their homes and ate together with glad and sincere hearts, 47 praising God and enjoying the favor of all the people. And the Lord added to their number daily those who were being saved.

People were added to the church daily and this is still the plan of God. Gods' strategy is to reveal His Son to the world. This is also why God gave His church the five-fold ministry gifts: apostles, prophets, evangelist, pastors, and teachers for equipping the believers. They are called to help grow and mature the body so they can minister reconciliation outside the four walls of the church building. The five-fold ministry gifts are to teach and train disciples to make disciples. (Ephesians 4:11).

The body of Christ is to be a witness of God's grace and His mercy in the earth so God's kingdom (family) can populate and dominate the earth. The church building is not just a place to gather and to come together to hear a good message and leave feeling good. The church building is supposed to be an equipping and training "center". The church is supposed to be a training center established by the Word of God, with Jesus being the Chief Cornerstone (Ephesians 2:20). The church building is where we meet to teach believers the principles of Gods kingdom and prepare them to go back out into the market place and be a witness and win souls. The Bible states in Luke 10:2, the harvest is ripe, but the labors are few. This clearly states something is wrong with the modern-day church when it comes to evangelism.

After all these years since Jesus rose from the dead, only one-fourth of the population of people living to date are a part of the family of God. Why is this? And the question is *who* do the other three-fourths belong to? Is satan winning the race for human souls? Is the kingdom of darkness growing stronger than the kingdom of God, which is the kingdom of light?

Also, why is it most major cities in America have more churches than any other institution? The number of lost souls out-number the number of Christians. Something is wrong! This is an outrageous assault and indictment on the kingdom of God. Don't think for one moment God is pleased with the church or Christianity as we know it today.

The body of Christ must get busy about the Fathers business and stop having Sunday morning "church" as usual. The church must began fulfilling the call to the great commission (See Matthew 28:16-10) before it's too late. We cannot afford to lose any more people, family members, love ones, friends, colleagues, communities, nations, etc., to the kingdom of darkness.

We have lost a lot of people (men, women, boys, and girls) to the devil and to other religions in the last century. But the people that know their God shall do exploits. We have to get busy and began reaching the masses with the good news of the gospel of the Lord Jesus Christ. Because if we don't, they will ultimately die and go to hell. We must do something and speak up now!

Note: Throughout this book the reapers are hereafter referred to as the body of Christ (believers). And the harvest is referred to those that are in the world without the knowledge of the saving grace of the Lord Jesus Christ (people, nations, mankind, souls, etc.).

Note: Hell is a place God never intended for mankind to go to. But because of a lack of knowledge, disobedience, and unbelief in the finished works of the Lord Jesus Christ. Hell has enlarged itself with people who have not heard nor received Jesus as their Lord and Savior.

II

The History and Fall of Mankind

Let's take a brief look at the history of mankind as it relates to salvation. In the book of Genesis 1:26-27, God says:

> [26] Let us make man in our image, after our likeness: and let them have dominion over the fish of the sea and over the fowl of the air, and over the cattle, and over all the earth, and over every creeping thing that creeps upon the earth. [27] So God created man in his own image, in the image of God created he him; male and female created he them.

The first man and woman, Adam and Eve were created in the very image and likeness of God. In His image meaning Adam and Eve were an exact replica and representation of God the Father in the earth *spiritually*. They lived in the Garden of Eden naked and unashamed.

[25]

The Old Testament is rooted in the fall of mankind. Romans chapter 5:12 talks about how through one man. *Adam* sin. Sin entered into the whole earth and death passed upon all mankind. This scripture explicitly states that mankind is born into sin. Every human being is born into a perpetual state of sin. Fallen beings through deception.

Deception is one of satan's greatest tools and strategies to defeat mankind. If satan can get people to believe a lie, then he has succeeded with his tactics. satan has and is still using deception to keep mankind in a fallen state. Blinded by darkness and blinded from the saving revelation knowledge of who Jesus Christ is.

In the garden of Eden, God gave Adam a specific commandment. And that commandment was to *not* eat of the tree of the knowledge of good and evil. Genesis 2:16-18 states:

> And the Lord God commanded the man, saying, of every tree of the garden thou mayest freely eat: [17] But of the tree of the knowledge of good and evil, thou shalt not eat of it: for in the day that thou eat thereof thou shalt surely die.

However, the serpent (satan) tempted Eve, Adam's wife to eat the forbidden fruit from the tree of knowledge of good and evil. The tree which God commanded them not to partake of. Eve then tempted Adam her husband to eat. And right after they ate the fruit. They both realized they had sinned against God and disobeyed His commandment.

This very act of disobedience caused sin and death to enter into the earth realm. They both were ashamed of their sin and knew they were naked, and the glory of God had departed from them. After which, God expelled them from the Garden of Eden to prevent them from eating from the Tree of Life. If they had eaten from the Tree of Life in their fallen state, they would not have been able to be redeemed. This is the doctrine of *"the fall"*. Genesis 3:1-13 states:

> Now the serpent was craftier than any of the wild animals the Lord God had made. He said to the woman, "Did God really say, 'You must not eat from any tree in the garden'?" [2] The woman said to the serpent, "We may eat fruit from the trees in the garden, [3] but God did say, 'you must not eat fruit from the tree that is in the middle of the garden, and you must not touch it, or you will die.'" [4] "You will not certainly die," the serpent said to the woman. [5] "For God knows when you eat from it your eyes will be opened and you will be like God, knowing good and evil." [6] When the woman saw that the fruit of the tree was good for food and pleasing to the eye, and also desirable for gaining wisdom, she took some and ate it. She also gave some to her husband, who was with her, and he ate it. [7] Then the eyes of both of them were opened, and they realized they were naked; so, they sewed fig leaves together and made coverings for themselves. [8] Then the man and his wife heard

the sound of the Lord God as he was walking in the garden in the cool of the day, and they hid from the Lord God among the trees of the garden. [9] But the Lord God called to the man, "Where are you?"

[10] He answered, "I heard you in the garden, and I was afraid because I was naked; so, I hid." [11] And he said, "Who told you that you were naked? Have you eaten from the tree that I commanded you not to eat from?"

[12] The man said, "The woman you put here with me—she gave me some fruit from the tree, and I ate it."

[13] Then the Lord God said to the woman, "What is this you have done?" The woman said, "The serpent deceived me, and I ate."

The word fall is used to describe the transition in which Adam and Eve fell from a state of innocence to a state of sin, shame, disobedience, and rebellion. When Adam and Eve fell into sin, sin and death entered the entire earth realm and into the hearts of every man, woman, and child born thereafter. Mankind was not supposed to ever die physically. But after the fall God sentenced both Adam and Eve to a life of physical death, and eternal damnation. Mankind was supposed to live spiritually and physically forever. A life like heaven on earth. A life with God without sin and without death. But because of their disobedience mankind was sentenced to a life of physical and spiritual death (Romans 5:12). Just think if Adam and Eve had not disobeyed and rebelled against God's commandment. Just think how glorious life could have been. The sin of disobedience was an outright disgrace. Thus, causing the whole human race to born into a perpetuate state of rebellion.

Adam and Eve fell out of covenant relationship and fellowship with God. But thank God mankind's relationship has now been restored through the shed blood of the Lord Jesus Christ. Because the shed blood of animals as noted all throughout the Old Testament was not sufficient enough for a sin sacrifice. The blood of animals could not pay for the wages of man's sin. Nor could it suffice the eternal corrupt soul of a sinner.

Death is what Adam and Eve deserved for disobeying God's commandment. However, death was not enough to cover the payment for sin. Only a perfect, spotless, sinless sacrifice offered in just the right way could pay for the sins of all mankind. Sin requires punishment and atonement for. Or else eternal death and permanent separation from God would prevail. Jesus was and is the perfect sacrifice. He came to offer a pure, complete, and everlasting sacrifice that removes, atones, and pays for eternal punishment and judgment.

The fall brought about corruption including humanism and human reasoning. satan, who is known for being the great deceiver, a liar, and the accuser of the brethren. Deliberately and strategically tricked Eve into reasoning with what God had said. And because Adam listened to his wife and took of the fruit of the tree of knowledge of good and evil. The whole earth was placed into a perpetual state of judgment. Issues and situations that would have never entered the Earth realm are now a part of the "curse" that was placed on Adam and Eve in the garden. Genesis 3:14-23 states:

> [14] and the Lord God said to the serpent, "Because you have done this, "Cursed are you above all livestock and all wild animals! You will crawl on your belly and you will eat dust all the days of your life.
>
> [15] And I will put enmity between you and the woman, and between your offspring [and hers; he will crush your head, and you will strike his heel."
>
> [16] To the woman he said, "I will make your pains in childbearing very severe; with painful labor you will give birth to children. Your desire will be for your husband, and he will rule over you."
>
> [17] To Adam he said, "Because you listened to your wife and ate fruit from the tree about which I commanded you, 'You must not eat from it,
>
> "Cursed is the ground because of you; through painful toil you will eat food from it all the days of your life.
>
> [18] It will produce thorns and thistles for you and you will eat the plants of the field. [19] By the sweat of your brow you will eat your food until you return to the ground, since from it you were taken; for dust you are and to dust you will return."

[20] Adam named his wife Eve, because she would become the mother of all the living.[21] The Lord God made garments of skin for Adam and his wife and clothed them.

[22] And the Lord God said, "The man has now become like one of us, knowing good and evil. He must not be allowed to reach out his hand and take also from the tree of life and eat and live forever."

[23] So the Lord God banished him from the Garden of Eden to work the ground from which he had been taken. [24] After he drove the man out, he placed on the east side of the Garden of Eden cherubim and a flaming sword flashing back and forth to guard the way to the tree of life.

Satan still uses manipulation and deception to draw people into disobedience, sin, and away from believing the truth. Just like he did when he deceived and manipulated Adam and Eve. He is still deceiving people every day, everywhere. He is still trying to prevent people from coming into the kingdom of God and from receiving a personal relationship with God through the Lord Jesus Christ. Satan knows the blood that Jesus shed on Calvary has the power to deliver a person from a fallen state and from a burning hell. He also knows his time is short because God has promised to sentence him and all the demonic angels to eternal damnation, in the lake of fire (*hell, hades*).

After the entire situation of the fall, God still did not go back on His original plan. Before the fall and before the foundations of the world and even before satan ever tempted Adam and Eve. God the Father, God the Son, and God the Holy Spirit had a divine meeting in heaven concerning the matter. All three came together in agreement to execute a redemptive plan of salvation for mankind. A redemptive plan that would permit mankind to populate the whole earth with people made in the image and likeness of God. God in His sovereignty predetermined that His original plan to have a family and a kingdom of people would be executed, by sending Jesus into the earth to be a sin sacrifice.

Mankind's redemption through belief in the redemptive work of the Lord Jesus Christ confirms God's plan. Not even Adam and Eve's sin could stop it. God was and is always thinking about the harvest of the world. Even before the devil tempted them. God was thinking about His relationship with mankind and their rightful position to have dominion and authority in the earth.

God created mankind in his own image,
in the image of God he created them;
male and female he created them.
Genesis 1:27

III

The Gospel must be Preached

The main theme for preaching the gospel is salvation through Jesus Christ. The New Testament Bible reveals the source of salvation through *faith* in Christ. People can be saved by faith from God's eternal judgment and from the consequences of eternal death in hell. Biblical salvation is God's *only* way of providing deliverance to mankind from sin and spiritual death.

Through repentance and faith in the finished works of Jesus Christ on the cross, it is of essences for believers to go preach and teach the gospel, so souls can be saved. John 3:36, states, "he that believeth on the Son hath everlasting life: and he that believeth not the Son shall not see life; but the wrath of God abides on him".

[33]

The plan of redemption allows mankind the much-needed relationship with God. It allows him to be able to come back to God with a state of holiness and right standing, as the elect body of Christ. There must be an urgency to go preach the gospel. Preach so people can be saved from a fallen state from which they are spiritually born into. Preach so the gospel can be reached in all the land, so mankind can be redeemed from the curse. And to be consummated into a right relationship and with God, via *"the way"* of Jesus Christ.

God is looking for those that are committed and obedient to His plan of salvation. God's people the church, the body of believers must be willing to go into the entire world and preach the kingdom of God so every man, woman, boy, and girl can have a chance to hear and be saved. Saved from eternal death in exchange for eternal life. Fellowship and relationship with God, is the goal. And for all to be a part of the great family of God.

Jesus makes a truly astounding claim for the activity of preaching. He maintains that the end of the world and His coming *again* awaits on the preaching of the gospel. Noting until the gospel has been preached everywhere, the end cannot come. (See Matthew 24:14; Mark 13:10). As soon as the gospel is preached everywhere and to everyone, then the end will come. God alone is the only one who knows the day and the hour of the end of the dispensation of saving *grace*. He knows it because He has pre-determined it in His eternal counsel. The time is fixed and the view on preaching's must run its course throughout the world.

All the things that are going to happen in the last days (*end-times*) and all the other signs of the end are secondary to the preaching of the gospel. Everything concerning the end-times is hinged on the gospel being preached. Therefore, the church must be *made* ready for the greatest harvest of souls ever. The glorious gospel of the kingdom must be preached and demonstrated with power and with God's love on display. The preaching of the kingdom of God and the gospel will give people the opportunity to hear the good news. And decide to receive Jesus Christ as their personal Lord and Savior. God's glory must be seen in all the earth before it's too late.

After hearing the gospel preached a person can then make a conscious decision to be born again into the family of God. God has given every person the freewill of choice. Therefore, it is up to everyone to receive Jesus as their own personal Lord and Savior on their own. Nobody can receive for another nor be made to believe or receive. Many have died and left this earth without ever hearing the gospel. And many have heard but have not responded to the invitation because of pride and disobedience. But thanks be to God. There are many souls that have made the decision to receive Jesus as their personal Lord and Savior and many have come into the kingdom of God.

Note: God's original plan for a family must be completed.

Jesus calls the preaching of the gospel, the preaching of the kingdom. It is the good news about the kingdom God. The kingdom of God is not of man. It is the kingdom of heaven and not of the world. It is spiritual, not earthly. The foundation of the kingdom is established in righteousness. The kingdom is the rule of Jesus Christ, the Holy Spirit, and the Word of God. To enter the kingdom, one must enter by faith through confession in Jesus Christ. The kingdom is established in the hearts of mankind. And there is peace in knowing that there is a heavenly citizenship, the forgiveness of sins, and fellowship with God.

The prosperity of the kingdom of God is the richness of salvation, that must be preached throughout the world before the end comes. The preaching of the cross is foolishness to those who are perishing. But God has chosen the foolish things of this world to confound the wise, and the weak things to confound the mighty. God's foolishness is always wiser than man's wisdom. And God's weakness is always stronger than man's natural strengthen. Insignificant and ridiculous as it may seem the preaching of the gospel is the only way into the kingdom of God. And God's Word in the only way the world will know Jesus saves.

The church mustn't miss out on the opportunity of the harvest of the world. Just making church membership is not enough. Church membership is not the same as going into the entire world to make disciples as Jesus mentioned in His closing message to His disciples, known as the *Great Commission*. See Matthew 28:16-20.

It's a dishonor if the church army doesn't fulfill its marching orders, given by the General, the Lord Jesus Christ, to "go" make disciples. (Mark 16:15). The Bible clearly states, there is only one way back to right standing with God. That way is through the cross, the blood, and the gift of salvation.

Through God wrapped up in the body of the Lord Jesus Christ. No other religion, prophet, preacher, teacher or evangelist can guarantee salvation. Jesus is the only one who died for all mankind and He is the only way to salvation and God the Father.

Jesus commanded His disciples to go into the entire world and preach the gospel. The key word is, "go". However, most churches today don't go as the bible commands. Rather, they sit by and remain idle. There are those unfaithful servants in Matthew 20:6 of whom Jesus said, "why stand ye here all day idle?" The most important duty of every Christian is to go soul winning. 2 Corinthians 5:10-11, for we must all appear before the judgment seat of Christ; that everyone may receive the things done in his body, according to that he hath done, whether it be good or bad. Every born-again believer has a responsibility to share the *good news* of the Lord Jesus Christ to the lost, so people can be forgiven and spend eternity in Heaven (God's Kingdom).

An alarming number of Christians are zealous to preach the gospel, but they don't know how. The way to be saved is to acknowledge Jesus as Savior for sin and receive Him as payment for sin. That's good news. Jesus died, was buried and rose from the grave for our justification. He took our sins upon Him. This is the inspired Word of God and the way in which we are to present the gospel.

Note: The great need in today's churches is preaching preachers who will teach their parishioners and congregants to be creative about soul winning.

The gospel can be presented in many ways besides preaching. It can be presented through plays, through singing, etc., as long as it represents the death, the burial, and the resurrection of the Lord Jesus Christ!

Romans 10:13-14 states, "For whosoever shall call upon the name of the Lord shall be saved. How then shall they call on Him in whom they have not believed? And how shall they believe in Him of whom they have not heard? And how shall they hear without a preacher?" Matthew 28:19-20 is commonly referred to as "The Great Commission". It states, we are to go and teach all nations, baptizing them in the name of the Father, and of the Son, and of the Holy Ghost: Teaching them to observe all things whatsoever Jesus has commanded. However, most believers fail to realize that there are two parts to the great commission. That is preaching the gospel and teaching new converts how to be soul winners.

A lot of Christians these days are doing good works. However, we mustn't get social work, social justice, humanitarian efforts and philanthropy mixed up with evangelism and spreading the gospel. Although these can be creative ways to getting the gospel to people. And at times it seems as if the they-go hand and hand. However, there must be a clear line of demarcation. Feeding the homeless, clothing the naked and other outreach mission types of ministries are not necessarily the same as evangelism nor is it the same as ministering the message of reconciliation.

Many churches and ministries are going out of their way doing good works, and teaching parishioners to do the same. This is not a bad thing. But far too many ministries are not operating from a standpoint of scripture as found in Matthew 25: 34-40 which states:

> [34]Then shall the King say unto them on his right hand, Come, ye blessed of my Father, inherit the kingdom prepared for you from the foundation of the world: [35]For I was a hungered, and ye gave me meat: I was thirsty, and ye gave me drink: I was a stranger, and ye took me in: [36]Naked and ye clothed me: I was sick, and ye visited me: I was in prison, and ye came unto me. [37]Then shall the righteous answer him, saying, Lord, when saw we thee a hungered, and fed thee? Or thirsty, and gave thee drink? [38]When saw we thee a stranger, and took thee in? Or naked, and clothed thee? [39]Or when saw we thee sick, or in prison, and came unto thee? [40]And the King shall answer and say unto them, verily I say unto you, in as much as ye have done it unto one of the least of these my brethren, ye have done it unto me.

These things ought to be done. However, it mustn't stop there. Because what if you feed someone today and they die tomorrow without having heard the gospel preached to them. Romans 10:14 says, "how then shall they call on him in whom they have not believed? And how shall they believe in him of whom they have not heard? And how shall they hear without a preacher?" The believer must go and tell them.

Testimony:

One ministry is reaching out to people via feeding and clothing distributions. This ministry involves preaching the gospel and getting people saved as well. The ministry believes, what good does it profit to feed someone a bowl of soup and provide them with some clothing, but fail to minister salvation to them. And to warn them of the wrath to come if they do not believe or reject Jesus as Savior.

Note:

Social work, social justice, and humanitarian efforts mixed with evangelism are also creative ways to getting the message of salvation and the gospel to people as well.

He that winneth souls is wise!

Proverbs 11:30

IV

Evangelism and Dispersion of Labors into the World

Evangelism is a New Testament methodology. It is imperative that the body of Christ *"labors"* fulfill the great commission, and assist Jesus in winning as many people into the kingdom of God. Evangelism methods are simple, easy, and effective that every believer can learn. Evangelism methods are also strategic in preparing labors to glean the harvest of souls. Winning people from the kingdom of darkness and from the kingdoms of this world; into the kingdom of light is effective evangelism.

The office of an evangelist is one who proclaims the gospel and helps equip, nourish, and edify the body of Christ to do the same. An evangelist is a

[41]

leadership position. However, the evangelist was never supposed to be just a ministry or office given to the church for itinerate ministry, conference speaking and Sunday morning preaching only. According to Ephesians 4:11-12, the evangelist is called alongside the other five-fold ministry gifts: apostles, prophets, *evangelist*, pastors, and teachers; to prepare, to train, and to equip believers; to do the work of ministry inside and outside the church building. The parishioners – "congregates" are the church. They are called-out to help God win the lost. And to help God establish His family in the earth. Likewise, the evangelist is called to help deploy effective labors into the vineyards of the world. These labors must be strategically trained, equipped, and made ready to handle the word of God with skill and boldness.

Evangelist is defined as:

- ❖ A preacher who is sometimes itinerants and often preaches at open air meetings.
- ❖ A preacher of the Christian gospel (the Kingdom of God).
- ❖ A person that is zealous for and advocates the Gospel.
- ❖ Another word for a revivalist.

Evangelism is defined as:

- ❖ The preaching or promulgation of the gospel Jesus Christ and doing the work of an evangelist.
- ❖ Missionary zeal, purpose, or activity.

Both definitions explain what evangelism is and what an evangelist does. However, any Christian believer can fit the description and category of an active evangelist within the contexts of the definition.

Sometimes, the regular minister of a church is called a *preacher* in a way that other groups would typically use the term pastor. In *most* churches the evangelist is the one who travels from church to church, spreading the gospel of Jesus Christ. Many preachers of various theological perspectives would call themselves evangelists because they spread the gospel.

The title evangelist is also associated with those who lead large meetings town to town, in tents, existing church buildings, or those who address the public on street corners preaching to people who pass by. Christians who specialize in evangelism are also often referred to as missionaries.

Note: The scriptures do not use the word *evangelism*, but they do use the word evangelist as used in Acts 21:8, Ephesians 4:11, and 2 Timothy 4:5.

Proclaiming the gospel is more than just preaching in a pulpit or in open air meetings. Proclaiming the gospel is when you *win* someone over to the Lord Jesus Christ through the message of the Word of God and make disciples at the same-time. Every Christian believer should be able to proclaim and minister the gospel. However, not all Christians are ordained by God to stand in the *office* of an evangelist. The office and the work are not to be confused. They are two different functions.

Far too long the role of the evangelist has been confined within the four walls of the church, exciting and stirring up believers with inspirational and sensational preaching. However, the church was never supposed to be relegated to a building or a meeting where people just gather to come hear the preached word, shout, get excited and run around the building.

The church, Greek word *ecclesia* was established so people would come hear the gospel of the kingdom and be *equipped* to do the work of ministry. The work of ministry includes church worship, administration, and governess. But the most important task is to be a witness and reconcile souls into God's kingdom. Churches, ministries, and ministers must begin to equip the body of Christ to go forth in the market place, with their families and friend, communities, etc., so the end-time harvest can be reaped. Pastors must begin to seek out anointed evangelist within the congregation that are able to train and equip the congregation.

Note: Training is key to effective evangelism.

The parishioners are the church. They are the called-out ones, called to help God win the lost and to help establish His family in the earth. Christians are to become effective labors and deployed labors. They are to be sent into the vineyards of the earth and reap the harvest of souls. These labors must be strategically trained, equipped, and ready to handle the word of God with skill and boldness. For the Bible says, the harvest is ripe, but the labors are few (Luke 10:2).

The bottom line hasn't changed in the 21st century church. God's heart beat continuously longs for souls to come into the kingdom in these last days. The pastor's responsibility is to make sure congregates are being feed the word of God, so they can mature and grow into seasoned disciples and able to make disciples. It was never the vision, passion, or mission of Jesus Christ for the church to just make members. People need to be taught how to love God with all their heart and their neighbor as themselves. They are to be taught how to live right, and receive all the benefits that come along with salvation, such as healing and prosperity. However, this was never supposed to be the all-inclusive package to the churches mission.

If the church doesn't arise up out of its sleep and slumber. And began to evangelize and go out into the highways and bi-ways and compel people to come to Jesus. Many lost souls may never be won. The church must minister reconciliation to the lost and all cost. There must be a burning passion for soul winning and there must be willing labors to go forth. People are dying and going to hell every day. They must know Jesus as their Savior. That He died for them and that it is Gods will for them to be saved, *born again*. Not only must they be told that God loves them. But they must be discipled and taught about the new birth. It is the churches responsibility and the responsibility to *not* ignore the call nor abort the *Great Commission*.

Ministry outside the four walls is a must if the church is to grow and save people from eternal damnation. The focus of the church must return to its first love Jesus and love for the lost. If the first century church was able to be successful in taking the gospel to all the ends of the earth. Then how much more is the 21st century church able, with all the vast array of technology? This does not mean everyone is called to be an evangelist or missionary. However, God has given every believer the ministry of reconciliation. (See II Corinthians 5:18-19). On the day of judgment, the bible says, that every born-again believer will have to give an account of the things he or she has done on the earth. This includes the ministry of reconciliation. (Romans 14:12).

To be honest the church has done a poor job of equipping the saints to do the work of an evangelist. And a poor job of sending labors into the vineyards (harvest fields, world, etc.). Parishioners must get engaged in evangelism. The Bible says, in Proverbs 11:30, "the fruit of the righteous is a tree of life; and he that wins souls is wise".

In the beginning of church history, the church was mobile and effective in prayer and soul winning. Many new converts were birthed into the kingdom of God on a daily basis. Many were converted from Judaism to Christianity. The church is the most world's powerful movement since the history of mankind. The new birth is an experience that every person on earth should be allotted to experience. Or at least given the chance to hear the gospel. Because if they do not hear, believe, and receive Jesus Christ as their Savior. They will die and spend eternity in hell. We all have a part to do and if we don't get back to the basics of reconciliation, on judgment day many well intended works of the church and outreach events will be burnt up and not counted as righteousness. It was never the will of the Father to reach out and feed a person and not share the gospel to them. (Matthew 7:23).

There seems to be a misconception within the body of the Christ, that Christians are to only go about their daily lives and let their light shine so others my see their good works and be drawn to the light. However, the Bible talks about letting others behold your good works so that *God* will be glorified! In the book of Matthew it says, "Let your light so shine before men, that they may see your good works, and glorify your Father which is in heaven" (Matthew 5:15-17). The Bible does not say that the believer is to remain silent and *just* shine until the unbeliever asks them about their salvation. Good works can be a witness. But the most effective witness is when a believer opens-up their mouth and minister reconciliation to those that don't know Jesus. New and mature believers should be compelled to share their testimony and the gift of salvation with others regardless of fear or intimidation.

When looking at other religions in various regions and the difference between salvation God's way and the world's way is that other religions tend to focus on "good works" as the *only* way to right standing with God. This is wrong, and deceiving. Even in certain so-called Christian circles this is happening. God has provided His grace and mercy in the New Testament through repentance and confession. (See Romans 10:8, 9, 10, 13). The Old Testament is the shadow of things to come. However, in the New Testament, Jesus is the sin sacrifice. Jesus Christ the Messiah has come to redeem all mankind from every nation, tribe, and tongue. All are welcome to believe and to receive new life and salvation through the Jesus Christ - *new birth*.

The eternal gathering of the harvest of souls has to be so vast that it consists of many people from all walks of life, all nations, people groups, cultures, classes, nationalities, races, colors, and creeds. So far, the distribution of the gospel of Jesus Christ and the kingdom of God has only reached various countries and continents in proportions of less than 50% with America being the leaders in the numbers of Christians evangelization. However, fifty percent in still not good enough, with an alarming rate of 50% being left in the dark. The communication of the Christian faith must reach out to new geographical areas and cultures before it's too late.

Note: There are no special formulas to becoming a soul winner. However, effective evangelism starts with a burning desire, passion, and perspective to see souls saved. In ministry it begins in the pulpit with leadership that is equipping and training congregates to comply with the move of evangelism. Because evangelism is well pleasing to God.

The harvest is ripe, but the labors are few.

Luke 10:2

$\mathcal{V}$

Gods Strategic Planning and Methodology to Soul Winning

God's strategic plan for salvation is very loving and heartfelt. His plan is based on the premise and foundation found in the book of Mark chapter 16:15-18, known as "The Great Commission". Here is where Jesus says, to His disciples, go into the entire world and *preach* and *teach* and *baptize* all people, so that people can be saved and come into the kingdom of God.

Now that the payment for sin has been paid for through the shed blood of Jesus Christ; the mandate of the great commission must be fulfilled. It is up to the church to win as many people as possible into the kingdom of God in these last days. However, the question is how do we continue the mandate and execute the commission in modern day vernacular?

God's strategy was initiated when He sent Jesus His Son, into the earth to be a ransom, and a propitiatory for the sins of mankind. According to John 3:16, "God so loved the world, that he gave his only begotten Son and whosoever believeth in Him should not perish but have everlasting life". This solidifies and confirms just how much God loves humanity and just how much He intendeds on reaping a harvest of souls for His kingdom. With over two thousand years gone by since Jesus walked the earth and since His crucifixion. God is still waiting for the precious fruits of the harvest to come to full fruition.

Jesus is and was the lamb slain before the foundations of the world. He was sent to restore mankind back to a rightful position and covenant relationship with God, through His death, burial, and resurrection. Jesus's coming into the world was enough to destroy all the works of sin and all the works of the devil. In the book of John 10:10, Jesus says, the thief (the devil) comes to steal, to kill, and to destroy. But Jesus says, He, Himself came that we might have life and life more abundantly. Jesus Christ blood reconciles mankind back to God and guarantees mankind all the covenantal rights that were lost in the Garden of Eden before the fall of Adam and Eve.

Note: Salvation for humanity was made possible for past, present, and future generations. Jesus paid it all on Calvary. His body was offered for all mankind sins and failures. Through His blood we can all be made free from sin.

According to John 3:16, we do not have to perish. If we believe on Jesus Christ, we will have everlasting life! This solidifies and confirms just how much God loves humanity and just how much He intends on reaping a harvest. With over two thousand years gone since Jesus walked the earth. We can rest assured that God is still waiting for the precious harvest of souls that will not perish but last throughout eternity.

So, why aren't more people coming into the kingdom of God? And what is the fivefold ministry gifts doing to get the job done? And why is it, that most church meetings are centered on all kinds of programs and events, instead of equipping believers to win souls, and make disciples? I'll tell you why. We have forgotten the importance of soul winning. We have gotten so full and fat off the word of God, that we are not as concerned about the masses of lost souls anymore. We tend to focus on individual blessings that come with our *own* quest of salvation, rather than the people in the world who are dying every day without making Jesus Christ their Lord and Savior.

While the harvest is out there rotting (*perishing*); and with all that's going on in the world. Gods' methodology for the church is to go into the entire world, outside the four walls of the church building. And tell people of His saving Grace.

Everywhere we go we are to walk in love and use wisdom. Because majority of the people that we come in contact with may never come through the doors of a church building to hear the salvation message and be given the opportunity to be saved.

There is no other religion or demon in hell that has the strongest influence, authority, power, or voice in the earth than the church. Majority Christians living in the United States of America alone have the power to get the job done. The regional distribution of Christians throughout the world is an indication that the gates of hell cannot and will not prevail against the church. People must open their mouths, get trained in evangelism, and go share and tell others about the goodness of God. Every human being needs to know what God has provided for them through Jesus Christ.

Note: *New converts are some of the best soul winners for Jesus!*

My Testimony

Nine months after receiving Jesus Christ as my Lord and Savior. I was so excited I joined the evangelism team at the church I attended. I also attended early morning prayer meetings at 5 am Monday through Friday. I started going out to witness to the lost every Saturday mornings, on the streets of Detroit, Michigan with the evangelism team. I wanted everyone I came in contact with to experience the New Birth and to experience the joy that I had received from being delivered from sin, depression, and a host of other things.

After being faithful in prayer and serving on the evangelism team for three years (street witnessing, door to door evangelism). The team leader and evangelist promoted me (which was really God promoting me, because promotion comes from the Lord) to team leader and minister of the word of God. I became the team captain to an all-girls youth home facility. Ministering to young ladies ages 12-18 on maximum lock down. God did some wonderful and miraculous things in that facility.

I keep reiterating, the church must get into position and go tell the masses about the saving grace of the Lord Jesus Christ. We must prepare to go into the market place, the neighborhoods, the community, the highways, the bi-ways, the highest mountains, and to the lowest valleys to proclaim Jesus Christ is Lord, before it's too late. We don't want to miss this great window of opportunity. The greatest opportunity is to be able to minister reconciliation and salvation to a lost and dying world. I have no doubt in my mind that the great commission won't be fulfilled. I believe we are living in the great times. And the great commission *will* be fulfilled throughout all the earth. But we must prepare!!!!

God's strategic plan and methodology has not changed and won't change. He remains the same yesterday, today, and forever. He wants an earthly and heavenly family so much that He has ordained and predetermined in His heart to raise up labors, reapers, and harvesters to assist Him in these last days.

Jesus gave the church the strategy and the greatest responsibility there is in the entire world. So that every man, woman, boy, and girl can be given an opportunity to be saved. Those that are chosen by God are chosen to live for God and with God throughout eternity. The chosen must be part-takers of this great end-time gathering. The *ecclesia,* the church must prepare and be made ready as God's end-time army. An army of generals that will carry out the great commission.

Gods' methodology for the church, is that every believer assists Him in making disciples as well. Every believer has a worldwide ministry in helping God make disciples for the kingdom's sake. Christ is the head of the church and it is His desire to bring mankind back to his original state like in the garden. And like it was intended from the beginning of time before the fall of Adam and Eve.

Note: It is God's plan for every believer to help Him make disciples. Let's not be so busy gathering believers together for conferences, seminars, and believer's meetings that we forget about the harvest and the great commission.

Soul winning should be fun and creative. However, it requires practice and tactfulness. With correct training, teaching, and equipping reapers can be equipped with the essential tools and knowledge needed for effective evangelism. This kind of teaching is not being done in your average local assembly (church) today. Most churches or ministries don't even have a soul winning team. This is not to be judgmental or critical. I'm just stating a fact.

Having the kind of testimony that glorifies God for being an effective witness and getting someone saved and filled with the Holy Spirit is what every believer should have. Being skillful at doing the work of the ministry. It is possible, and very achievable to be soul winner. Evangelism is not supposed to be relegated to a Sunday afternoon church event or once a week event. Evangelism is a lifestyle and every believer must begin to think and act like it.

There needs to be more teachings and workshops focused on strategic methodologies on how to gather the harvest. The end-time harvest of souls must be won with compassion, passion, signs, wonders, and miracles following according to Mark, chapter 16. The church must prepare and get ready because Jesus is coming back one day soon. He is getting ready to unleash a holy anointing of repentance on the hearts of people that don't know him. He has already started breaking down barriers.

Racial barriers, denominational barriers, class barriers, political barriers and the list goes on. God is exposing and breaking down the hearts of mankind so nothing can hinder the flow of the Holy Spirit in these last days. He is preparing the hearts of His people both inside and outside the church building. The Bible says in the last days God will pour out His Spirit upon all flesh (Joel 2:28). The sinner must know in these last days that there is a God and that He loves them, and cares for their eternal soul salvation. Satan the god of this world satan has blinded the eyes of the *unbeliever* for far too long. Many Christians attend church services week after week without being fully aware of the masses that are dying and going to hell, because no one has taken the time to tell them about the Lord Jesus Christ.

The church was never supposed to be a place of entertainment. The church building is supposed to be designed as a place of refuge, a place of healing, and *equipping*. The "church building" is supposed to be designed in the spirit of Christ. It is to be a place where the believer comes together to learn of Him, be equipped for Him, and released to do the work of the ministry. This is the bottom-line! Work to win and save souls (the harvest). The desire of God is to see the church buildings all over this world filled with the vision and the mandate of the great commission.

Before Jesus left this earth and descended to heaven as described in Matthew, chapter 28, it was His desire to have people come into the full revelation knowledge of what their role is in helping Him to reap the harvest. The Bible says that God wishes that none should parish (2 Peter 3:9). The body of Christ must get busy and do to work. Don't misunderstand there needs to be preaching, praising, and worshipping God in church services. However, the facts remain, and statistics show that most Christian church services are geared towards exciting the people more so than equipping the people.

After most church services the people leave the building not willing or equipped to work for God. This type of Sunday morning worship must cease. People are dying and going to hell while we continue to just have "church". Enough is enough! How long will we stay as mere babes and not develop into a mature, seasoned, witness for Jesus Christ? The plan of God must be enforced. For there is no other way for the lost. But for believers to go tell them of His saving grace?

In the book of Acts, chapter one versus eight, Jesus says to the believers that were assembled in the upper room waiting for the full manifestation of the Holy Spirit. He said, behold I will give you power to be a witness for Me in Samaria, Judah, and unto the uttermost parts of the earth. This is a mandate that the early church had to fulfill. They knew what they were supposed to do as a collective body of believers. Through their obedience many people were saved and baptized with the Holy Spirit as they went forth and preached the kingdom of God.

Somehow or the other for the past two thousand years the body of Christ has gotten stuck behind the four walls. The church has forgotten what the purpose of receiving the Holy Spirit was for. It is very clear why Jesus sent the Holy Spirit according to Acts 1:8. The Holy Spirit was sent to empower believers to be a witness. Many have been saved and many are still being saved. However, in comparison to the first century church there's still more people dying and going to hell than being saved from hell.

The revival that broke out on the day of Pentecost caused thousands to be saved. In one service over three thousand souls were saved. The 21st century church must get back to its *main* mission and function. The church has to think in terms of winning the lost at cost. In some parts of the world and even in third world nations like Africa and India millions are attending crusades and hundreds of thousands are being saved. But this is still not enough. How many leave the crusades and go make disciples? This is what is needed. This is the whole crust of the matter. Many are being saved to attend church and become church members. And church membership should not be the reason for the church building. Yes, church membership is important.

Membership services is the way to the believer in all aspects of life. The Bible says not forsaking the assembling together (Hebrews 10: 25). This is how believer grow. The Bible also says believers are to preach the word, get souls saved, lay hands on the sick, *and* make disciples.

A disciple is a student. The student in these last days must be taught the word of God, trained how to be a witness, and then go out and make disciples. One of the requirements for church growth is a sincere desire to reach outside the four walls of the church building. To reach out to those in need of salvation.

Note: It is noted that many churches do not grow simply because they lack a desire and vision to grow. Many leaders are comfortable behind the pulpits on Sunday mornings preaching a Sunday morning message and teaching a mid-week bible study.

In the last decades in America some churches have modeled the "cell church" concept. Cell church growth has really been the *new wave* for outreach ministry for many congregations. The cell methodology is designed to meet once a week at designated homes of parishioners from local congregations. The meetings usually consist of prayer, Bible study, and fellowship. Believers are encouraged to bring new people from the community to the cell meets who would otherwise not attend a Sunday morning church service. These cell meetings consist of believers and unbelievers congregating together in homes to meet the needs of the community outside the four walls of the church with hope of bringing those that are not saved into the kingdom of God. *Note,* this is how the 1st century church met in the book of Acts.

Building relationships with people is another sure *method* to becoming an effective witness. Especially with people who may be hostile towards the gospel message. For example, people of other worldly religions, such as Muslims, Buddhist, Hindus, atheists, etc... However, tactfulness must be used. Be prepared to build relationships and befriend people that have *no* knowledge of the Christian faith. People in political offices and people from every walk of life and nationality need to sense and feel the love of God from those that call upon the name of the Lord. Sometimes just being nice and friendly is one of the greatest tools for effective evangelism. And can open doors to the gospel. Ways in which you can be-friend and build relationships are:

- Be polite
- Be kind
- Try to be likable
- Reach out to those in need
- Invite non-Christians to events with you
- Take co-workers out to lunch
- Married couple dinner dates with other married couples from other background, nationalities, and religion.
- Learn other ethnic group culture and ways. Don't just hang around the people that look like you and think like you.

- Get from outside the four walls of the church.
- Take care of someone in need.
- Sow into the lives of others
- Be communicable and approachable

Always remember to minister from the bible and never your opinion. The word of God is what convicts' people of their sins and brings them into repentance. When witnessing to family, friends, and love ones remember if they reject your message, they're not necessarily rejecting you; as much as they're rejecting the truth of the gospel of the Lord Jesus Christ. Therefore, don't take it personal. Keep witnessing and winning souls for the kingdom!

The New Testament urges believers to speak the gospel clearly, fearlessly, graciously, and respectfully whenever an opportunity presents itself (see Colossians 4:2-6, Ephesians 6:19-20, and 1 Peter 3:15). Throughout most church history, Christianity has been spread evangelistically, though various methods between Christian communities, and denominations. Evangelism, apologetics, and apostolic ministry often go hand in hand. Evangelism and apologetics can be seen in the United States, where door to door evangelism is the prospect in which an unbeliever is challenged to receive Jesus Christ as their Lord and Savior.

The evangelist wherein falls into the role of an apologist in defense of the faith with the hope winning souls. However, there are certain habits that soul winners possess. For instance, soul winners are spiritually prepared.

- They walk closely with Christ and maintain a consistent devotional life.
- They are active in their churches and are members in good standing.
- They attend worship and Sunday school and study their Bibles regularly.

They are trained.

- Soul winners have been trained in one or more gospel presentation strategies such as faith and sharing Jesus without fear, grow.
- They serve as trainers or mentors and model soul winning before others.
- They have marked New Testaments and are able to express the central truths of the gospel in simple and understandable fashion.
- They use tracts and other printed gospel materials to enhance their presentation.

They share Christ anytime and anywhere. And they are open to share Christ outside the church building and in the market place (See Places to Evangelize and Appendix C).

Soul winners are adaptable in their presentation of the gospel. Most do not rely on mechanical or canned gospel presentations. They each have developed their own style which is:

- personal and conversational
- uses of own language and illustrations

- witnessing encounter unique and different.

Soul winners see their interactions with other people as divine appointments. Therefore, they begin each day with a sense of expectation.

- They feel a divine sense of mission.
- They see themselves as instruments of God's grace to others.
- They seek to make the most of their encounter with others by purposely initiating and leading the conversation into the spiritual area.

Soul winners do not worry about the results. They realize that they cannot save anyone. People come to Christ only through the work of the Holy Spirit.

Soul winners are involved in church evangelism programs but are not limited by them.

Soul winners are active in their local churches. Most are involved in their church's ongoing visitation and evangelism training programs. But they do not limit themselves to sharing Christ only during church-sponsored activities.

- They see every moment of every day as an evangelistic opportunity.
- Soul winners also seek to reproduce themselves in others. Most mentor or train others through evangelism programs.

Soul winners pray consistently for opportunities to share Christ with others

- Soul winners pray for those with whom they have witnessed.
- They pray for those with whom they have not yet witnessed.
- They pray for divine appointments and witnessing opportunities.

It's ok to use various methods of presenting the gospel. However, we must never stray away from the fundamental Biblical truths. And that is the gospel saves, not eloquent words. If a lost sinner won't obey the gospel of Jesus Christ, then nothing else will persuade them. It's not human wisdom that convicts a sinful heart. It's the Word of God that does the conviction.

Also, every soul winner must claim the Lord's promises. Jesus said that he would be with us, whenever we go soul winning. In Matthew 28:19-20, He says, "Go ye therefore, and teach all nations, baptizing them in the name of the Father, and of the Son, and of the Holy Ghost: Teaching them to observe all things whatsoever I have commanded you: and, lo, I am with you always, even unto the end of the world. Amen." Jesus also promised to be with us, in power, as we go. What an Awesome God!

However, if you are afraid and think you cannot be an effective soul winner. Keep in mind that the Gospel is the message, and the Holy Spirit will be with you every step of the way. This is all we need to win people to Christ. You don't need to be eloquent or have a Ph.D. to win souls. You don't need to be a theologian. All you need is to do is tell people how you received salvation. And share the word of God to them and trust the Holy Spirit will convict them and pierce their hearts and to do the rest.

Testimony:

There are many ways to approach people and introduce them to the gospel. Sometimes I ride the bus when my car is being serviced to look for opportunities to share my faith in Jesus. You'd be surprised how many people are receptive to listening. I have had people even refuse the message an me telling them about the gospel. But that's okay! Because it's through the Holy Spirit that a seed is planted. Most people will listen if you are tactful, nice, and loving. Yet some will ignore you. Others may even curse you. But those that believe and receive shall be saved.

It is recommended that you always go soul winning with someone else if you're going door to door or in a secluded area. Your safety is always first. Jesus said He would be with us if we go and He would also give us *wisdom*. There is a fine line between faith and foolishness. Therefore, never place yourself in harm's way or in danger. Always use common sense. Everyday there are opportunities to share the gospel as you go about your daily schedules. There are always opportunities to share Jesus Christ in the Marketplace.

Note: Street evangelism and door to door evangelism... one should always go with a partner and not by themselves.

In most cases street preaching is a great way to directly present the gospel to large crowds. It can seem very awkward, walking up to a stranger, and outright asking them if they have received Jesus as their Lord and Savior. However, for those who may be afraid to witness in such an aggressive manner, there are many helpful alternatives. One method I prefer is to talk with people about world events, or recent news events. As you progress through the conversation, at some point interject a statement about God. For example: If I'm talking with someone about the news, I'll say something like

... "It's a shame that there's so much killing in the world, the world sure needs God." This is my foot in the door, a launching pad to present the gospel. Oftentimes, people will agree with such a statement, and then you can guide the conversation along from there, with a gospel presentation.

Jesus died for all mankind and He took the punishment
for sin of all mankind upon His body.

Journal Notes for Soul Winning Tactics:

VI

What is the Harvest, Labors and Leadership Roles?

Who is the harvest and what is the harvest? When people mention harvest, they are usually referring to an increase in produce, money, wheat, hay, etc... However, as Bible believing born again Christians when we think of harvest the first thing that should come to mind is souls, *people*. We know the harvest in the New Testament refers to people and souls. However, there are three distinct types of harvest people. There are those who are oppressed, hungry, and those that are looking for the supernatural. These three distinct types and groupings will help you to understand and help you to get ready to reap and bring them into the kingdom of God.

There are also several reasons, seasons, types, and times when the harvest is more fruitful and ripe to gather in. Never let witnessing become a duty. Let it be done because of your love for God and out love for the lost. For God is not mocked whatever a man sows that is what he shall reap (Galatians 6:7). The first type of harvest is the oppressed. These people have been broken, hurt, wounded, in bondage, and destitute from life's misfortunes.

God's desire is for people to be set free and the only way freedom can truly come to an individual is by Jesus Christ. When a person accepts Jesus as their Lord and Savior, they have every right and privilege to be set free from oppression. Therefore, the church (the body of believers) must minister reconciliation to those who are oppressed. They must tell them about Gods love and His saving grace. They must tell people about the goodness of the Lord and about God's mercy and His desire to set them free. God's will, is to set the captives free (John10:10). His will is to also deliver those that are oppressed of the devil, through deliverance and by His strips on Calvary.

The second types of harvest people are those that are hungry. This type of harvest (person) is good ground to sow seeds of love, testify of God too, and ministry reconciliation to. Over in Africa worldwide crusades are breaking out and millions are coming to the Lord because of their hunger for the things of God. A hungry person is desperate, and a hungry person will do whatever takes to get to God. This is the best harvest to witness to. Out of the three types of harvest the hungry soul will eat up the word sown in their hearts they are the ones that are also passionate and excited about telling others what God has done for them once they receive Jesus as their Lord and Savior. The hungry soul makes the best witness as well.

The third types of harvest people are those that are seeking the supernatural. These people are looking for sign, wonders, and miracles. In this dispensation it is very imperative that the body of Christ become spiritually aware of the spiritual gifts that Jesus has given to the body of Christ. The body of believers must also have the revelation of how significant signs, wonders, and miracles are and how significant they are when manifested in the earth. This is so vital and so necessary and is the exact replication of the ministry of the Lord Jesus Christ. Jesus's earthly ministry was full of signs, wonders, and miracles. What an awesome ministry in demonstration to those that don't believe in getting them to become believers (Mark 16:17).

Who are the reapers? The reapers are born again spirit filled believers who have been discipled and trained to glean the harvest. The reapers can be also called labors, witnesses, ministers of reconciliation, and soul winners. Statistic shows that face of global evangelism has changes since the 20th century. The reapers are no longer just comprised of predominantly Protestants or Catholics however, 200,000 are Protestants and Catholic together and more than 60,000 are from third world countries (Tapia, 1993, p 4). So here you have third world missionaries (reapers) coming to the west to reap the harvest. God said that the harvest is so ripe, but the laborers are so few. Therefore, the world needs a revival to break out in the east and the west that will release the reapers and gather of the harvest.

For the body of Christ to be effective reapers they must live a lifestyle of holiness and a lifestyle that reflects the Word of God. Although, God can still use a person that is not living in the full maturity of holiness, however, that person's witness will not be as effective and consistent as someone who is living according to God's Word. The Bible says, that the body of Christ is the light of the world, so let your light shine before men so that they might see your good works and glory God (Matthew 5:14, 16). By letting your light shine which is the glory of God within causes those that are in darkness to behold the glory of God and want to be drawn towards the light. A Christian's lifestyle must be so filled with the love of God that the light men see in them is actual the light of Jesus shining and drawing man to Himself.

The believer (reaper, soul winner) is not to manipulate or coerce anyone into becoming a follower of Christ. As people began to watch the lifestyle of the believer it becomes the bait. Lifestyle evangelism just means that your whole life is surrendered to God and that it is your aim, ambition, approach, and accountability to point people to Jesus. As a reflection of Jesus' light, believer's help to authenticate the message of salvation by giving people opportunity to experience God's grace through your good deeds. And as your light so shines it will also reveal the truth, so people can hear and believe.

In addition, you can't argue someone into the Kingdom. However, only the Holy Spirit can change a person's heart. That's why you must walk in love when soul winning. Always remember when winning a sinner, the believer that walk-in love is most effective and has the greatest impact. It's grievous when Christians are not sensitive to the Holy Spirit in this area of walking in love amongst the unbeliever.

Acts 1:8 says, "but ye shall receive power, after that the Holy Ghost is come upon you: and ye shall be witnesses unto me both in Jerusalem, and in all Judaea, and in Samaria, and unto the uttermost part of the earth." This power is necessary to be an effective reaper. The 21-century reaper must be endowed with power from on high to win this lost and perverse generation. The power that the reaper must tap into is the power of the Holy Spirit, because no one is able to win the lost within his or her own power. The Holy Spirit is the third person of the Trinity and He is the one that Jesus sent to help the body of Christ to carry out the great commission.

The believer (reaper) is to make the most of every opportunity and God will always confirm His word with signs following (Mark 16:20). The sign following is when a person gives their heart and life over to the Lord Jesus Christ and becomes a born-again believer. For this is the greatest miracle of all is when a man, woman, boy, or girl gives their life over to God. Oh, what joy it is being newly saved and born again. Remember the time when you first got saved? The joy that filled your heart as you invited the King of Kings and the Lord of Lords into your heart.

Likewise, the Bible says that the angels rejoice with great joy over a sinner that repents and turns to God (Luke 15:10). Therefore, it is imperative that churches and ministries raise up soul winners in these last days like no other time in church history. They must be equipped and trained on how to win souls and how to make disciples. God is going to hold the church accountable. The church of the living God must get back to basic when it comes to making disciples. And back to soul winning period.

The leadership must equip reapers for evangelism, which is a phenomenal task. Every leader must learn to trust and lean solely on the Holy Spirit in all things when it comes to equipping people to win souls. It's been recorded and stated numerous times that the leadership that depends on the Holy Spirit while going to the nations to preach and teach the gospel, can reach millions of souls for the Kingdom of God. The Holy Spirit can lead people and help restore people to God and the church.

Become a cutting-edge evangelistic leader and change agent for the church and the world is crucial as cultural changes accelerate. Church leaders need a new type of leadership that is based on preparing parishioners to reach people and make disciples for the Lord Jesus Christ. Leadership that not only preaches the gospel Sunday mornings in the pulpits, but, demonstrates that proclaims Jesus' mission to the world.

We need evangelistic leaders who are change agents for the Church and for the society as well. We need churches that grow through conversion. Evangelistic leadership is built on mentoring as displayed by the Lord Jesus Christ for his disciples. He mentored in small groups, he chose the men he would mentor, and he taught them on his timetable with the lessons he knew they needed to hear. After equipping them, he commanded them to impact the world with His teachings. This is challenging yet an encouraging approach. This mirrors the perfect execution Jesus used of bringing the hard truth, while balancing it with grace.

Soul winning is the most important concept for the church of our Lord Jesus Christ. It is noted that the Azusa Street Revival was the catalyst for Pentecostalism and evangelism. The Holy Spirit came like on the day of Pentecost to impart gifts and to infill with the Holy Ghost with the evidence of speaking in other tongues. Yet, without the wooing of the Holy Spirit upon men's hearts to be saved and to experience the born-again experience, then speaking in tongues would be in vain. According to Hyatt (2006) the Azusa Street Revival was a 20th century revival of biblical proportions that would hopefully result in world evangelism and usher in the Second Coming of Christ (p. 2).

The revival itself went throughout the world many we're being born again just as fast as they were being filled with the Holy Ghost. Because of the revival it is noted that many missionaries were birthed out of the revival and many took the gospel too other nations outside of America. While preaching and teaching the good news many were baptized in the Holy Spirit with the evidence of speaking in other tongues. The revival prepared the way for salvation of many souls and the birth of many assemblies and churches of over fifty million Pentecostals worldwide (Horton, 2006).

Note: The potent symbolic activity of the Holy Spirit with power to be a witness was and is the evidence of speaking in other tongues (See Book of Acts, Chapters 1-2).

We have to be very careful to not get discouraged. Always remember we are planting seeds. Even if the person you are ministering to does not receive Jesus Christ on the spot. We are co-labors with the Holy Spirit who will bring conviction to every person ministered to. 1 Corinthians 3:6-9 states:

> I have planted, Apollos watered; but God gave the increase.
> [7] So then neither is he that planteth anything, neither he that watereth; but God that giveth the increase. [8] Now he that planteth and he that watereth are one: and every man shall receive his own reward according to his own labor. [9] For we are laborer's together with God: ye are God's husbandry, ye are God's building.

VII

Places to Evangelize

There are so many ways and places to minister reconciliation, and to evangelize, and witness. The Bible says, those that are in the body of Christ are the light of the world and a light that sits on a hill that cannot be hidden (Matthew 5:14). Therefore, everywhere Christians go they are supposed to bring light into dark places. This is really a wonderful thing. Think back to when you first got saved. Do you remember the people God used to light your world? Can you remember the people that witnessed to you with their light shine bright, so you could see the Jesus in them?

There are many ways to win the lost and to carry out the great commission. Get your message and share your message with as many receptive people as possible, let them come to you not you to them. High-traffic areas good for evangelism might include downtown business districts, street fairs or farmers' markets, and college campuses. Avoid evangelizing around churches of other faiths and other places that might be contentious or difficult.

Invite neighbors into your homes. You can also host a community group on a regular basis that is not primarily focused on a study but on living out the gospel among unbelievers. You can host neighborhood block parties or activities for your neighbors (in my case, I have two buses who stop in front of my house). In addition, you can greet the mailman, garbage collectors, UPS person, or anyone else and leave with them information about the gospel. Finally, consider your workplace a mission outpost for the greater portion of your week and turn it into a mission amongst people who have the most access to you (outside your family).

Always use good judgment and be led by the Spirit of God. It might be a great idea to evangelize outside a concert on a Friday night, if you can pull it off, or it might just lead to arguments. Always make sure to follow any solicitation laws in the area and abide instructions from business and property owners who might want you to move on. Be courteous and leave. Malls and shopping centers are excellent places to evangelize the lost. Starting conversations with people is one way to get people to transition from the natural to the spiritual.

Some basic evangelism techniques and places that can be used as a platform or substituted pulpit can be done in many forms and fashions and at various times. For instance, below is a list of ways and methods to gather the harvest:

- Para-church evangelism groups (going out in teams)
- Individual evangelism door to door
- The office
- In a restaurant
- On a plane
- Over the phone
- Anywhere the opportunity exists.
- One-on-one evangelism
- Bus stop ministry
- Home visitations
- Distribution of tracts
- Evangelistic ministry through media tapes, CD's and DVD's
- Nursing home ministry
- Hospital ministry
- Music, telephone
- Drama
- Prison ministry
- Open street rallies
- Tent meetings
- Airplane evangelism

- World Wide Web – Blogs, Online Church Meetings
- Social Media Ministry
- 24-hour prayer line

(See Appendix C).

One of the most challenging evangelistic endeavors is what is called street evangelism. Approaching total strangers and explaining the gospel to them. When many people think of evangelism, this is often precisely what they have in mind—and they are intimidated by it. This kind of evangelism may be intimidating, but it also rewarding. There are people who exist outside of the sphere of Christian influence, and unless they hear the gospel from a stranger, they are likely not going to hear it at all. Many encounters are with people completely outside of the faith, unfamiliar with Christendom, and ignorant of the basics of the gospel (Jesus died in the place of sinners).

A few tips to getting started with evangelism outside the four walls of the church building is to always have a chosen location. The more people the better, because of greater opportunities for a greater harvest. For instance, evangelism on college campuses is a great way to win souls. Students often have free time and are often open to talking about the gospel. Likewise, have groups that go out to
hospitals, outdoor malls, and subways, where lots of people congregate.

Starting the conversation is the hardest part. Usually begin by introducing yourself and ask if they are familiar with the Bible or what Christians believe. Then make the jump to the gospel. Unlike relational evangelism (with friends, co-workers, neighbors, etc.) cold evangelism is a one-shot deal. Eventually you must make the jump to the gospel. Explain the gospel and any questions they ask—from why Christians do not believe in evolution, to what about the crusades—and answer with the gospel. A short gospel presentation includes who God is (creator and holy), who people are (sinful and in need of a savior), who Jesus is (God in flesh, sinless, substitute for sinners, who rose from the grave), and what we must do in response (turn from sin and believe the gospel in faith).

Every believer should have an evangelism strategy or plan for personally carrying out the Great Commission. Good stewardship of the gospel means that we must see how we can "do the work of an evangelist" in every "place" of our lives. We should be competent and opportunistic in every place because "becoming all things to all men" means you will be meeting all kinds of men and women, especially those not like you. If your evangelism is limited to the refined sinners who are within arm's reach of church building, you will reach a very small number of people and neglect the thrust of the Great Commission.

We must go into the entire world. That means depth and not just breadth. While the traditional mode of evangelizing in the first place has been "door-to-door evangelism," there are certainly other ways to utilize your home as a mission outpost for the kingdom.

Pray ye therefore to the Lord of the harvest, that he will send forth laborers into his harvest.
Matthew 9:38

VIII

Missions Ministry

The ministry of missions should be strongly advocated. The desire should be to equip others to go out into the highways and bi-ways to preach the gospel and to continue to support the vision that Jesus has for His church. The Great Commission is where Jesus commanded His disciples and church to go into the entire world and preach the gospel (Mark 16:15). Sponsoring, supporting, doing missions, outreach, and evangelistic endeavors is something every believer should have a passion for.

In many missionary settings, the missionary is allotted time to minister and get acquainted with and bond with those they feed, clothe, and nourish. They bond with the tribes and or people groups they minister to. They usually are able to also disciple as many new converts as they can. In most cases this methodology works best during permanent, long term, and some short-term mission trips. However, the average Christian isn't called to the mission field. So here you have another scenario and problem within the body of Christ. Because only a few are chosen to the mission field. However, this is not an excuse to not being effective with everyday evangelism.

Many people and nations are open to the gospel and many are *not*. But it's still up to the Christian to be open to share the gospel with anyone. Evangelism training is essential and necessary to reaching the lost in these last days. The Christian experience must be shared and politely offered to those that are blinded to the spiritual ramifications of not being "saved" and the eternal consequences of not knowing Jesus as Lord and Savior. Projects must be launched and implement to teach and train parishioners how to implement various outreach and evangelistic *mission outreaches within the community.*

The call to missions is not necessary a call to do international missions nor the call to be an apostle. Missionaries often travel to areas or to people groups where Jesus is not yet known. They frequently take on an evangelistic role. The apostolic *calling* is *not* necessarily the same as a missionary. It is a misinterpretation to equate them the same. There are many who serve in missions, church planting, and ministry development who have an apostolic calling and serve as an apostle. But their primary duty is *not* evangelism.

The nations of the world are rich especially in the 10/40 window of the world which is located in North Africa and throughout the Middle East to China. This area is also the least reached area of the world for the Lord Jesus

Christ. The call to missions is to preach and teach the Gospel of reconciliation to those that have not heard and to bring good tidings to those who need to know about Gods saving grace. The life of missions is something God is calling everyone within the local church community to do. Even if the believer never travels outside the country. They must be able to witness within the communities and world they live in.

Note: Every born-again believer should have a burning desire to be a witness wherever they go. The call to missions does not necessarily mean one must pack up and go live in an indigenous village, town, country, and/or nation to promote the kingdom. But the life and the call of missionaries are clearly meant to accelerate the gospel in other nation's whether it be long term or short-term missions.

The bottom line is, the church in the 21st century is not necessarily missionaries, but should be missions driven. Leaders have to start equipping others on how to evangelize, and plant assemblies in their own localities. Therefore, making more disciples for all nations.

Every culture has its own ways and style of worship. Missionaries are no longer needed for conforming people to western ways of doing things. Just like the Apostle Paul when he went into other nations. He gave the people the gospel and equipped them and then went on his way to other cities, villages, and or towns. Not once in the bible does it mention that he conformed the people to his ideology. He preached Jesus and left it up to the people to worship in their own native style and language, so that God could be glorified, and it was done in spirit and in truth.

Most missionaries and mission's workers take a holistic approach to ministry and one must be able to meet the needs of the people whom God is sending them to. And minister in a way the people can receive it. Gone with the dinosaur, so to speak, are the days where missionaries go into other nations, countries, villages, etc. to conform natives to their cultural standards and ways. Mission assignments today is not predicated upon promoting cultural connotation but predicted upon the administration of the gospel of the Lord Jesus Christ and the kingdom of God.

Missions is the greatest commandment in the bible. And is meant to help proclaim the saving grace, love, compassion, and provisions of the Lord Jesus Christ throughout the earth. The life of missions according to Matthew 25:24-46, states:

> Then shall the King say unto them on his right hand, Come, ye
> blessed of my Father, inherit the kingdom prepared for you
> from the foundation of the world: For I was a hungered, and ye
> gave me meat: I was thirsty, and ye gave me drink: I was a
> stranger, and ye took me in: Naked, and ye clothed me: I was
> sick, and ye visited me: I was in prison, and ye came unto me.
> Then shall the righteous answer him, saying, Lord, when saw
> we thee a hungered, and fed thee? Or thirsty, and gave thee
> drink? When saw we thee a stranger, and took thee in? Or

naked, and clothed thee? Or when saw we thee sick, or in prison, and came unto thee? And the King shall answer and say unto them, Verily I say unto you, in as much as ye have done it unto one of the least of these my brethren, ye have done it unto me. Then shall he say also unto them on the left hand, depart from me, ye cursed, into everlasting fire, prepared for the devil and his angels: For I was a hungered, and ye gave me no meat: I was thirsty, and ye gave me no drink: I was a stranger, and ye took me not in: naked, and ye clothed me not: sick, and in prison, and ye visited me not. Then shall they also answer him, saying, Lord, when saw we thee a hungered, or athirst, or a stranger, or naked, or sick, or in prison, and did not minister unto thee? Then shall he answer them, saying, verily I say unto you, in as much as ye did it not to one of the least of these, ye did it not to me. And these shall go away into everlasting punishment: but the righteous into life eternal.

Mission work is a duty, and evangelism is *not* just an event. Evangelism is a lifestyle that every born-again believer must practice. Therefore, to truly fulfill one's purpose as a Christian one must always remember to be on a mission and to have a missionary mentality to be a witness wherever they go. The force of missions is being able to respond to the great commission. The great commission is the main goal and reason why Jesus died. Therefore, it's the churches responsibility and their *mission* to help

Jesus redeem mankind back to the Father and back to a state of righteousness, just like it was before Adam and Eve sinned in the Garden of Eden.

Ephesians 4:11-12 says, God gave some to be apostles; and some, prophets; and some, evangelists; and some, pastors and teachers; For the perfecting of the saints, for the work of the ministry, and for the edifying of the body of Christ. This is a direct correlation of what the five-fold ministry gifts (leadership) is supposed to be for. The five-fold church leadership is supposed to be equipping believers and, nations for the work of ministry. The work of the ministry is to be a witness throughout the entire world and make more disciples for the Lord Jesus Christ (Mark 16:15). It is to build God's kingdom.

I truly believe the purpose of the church is not just for fellowshipping and bible study. We are to assemble for the sole purpose of being equipped to live right, worship God, learn about the kingdom of God, and to advance the kingdom of God throughout all the earth.

To reach the unsaved and the lost the believer must have a life that is anchored in the word of God. They must also live a life that is consistent with the ways of the Lord Jesus Christ by living a life of prayer and true holiness. There must be a passion and a commitment for missions. For the missionary, there must truly be a call to fulltime ministry. In addition, they must have what Shibley (2001) calls "the mission's addiction". A passion that burns within the heart of those that have the missions' addiction, is that they think like God and act like God. They are compelled to minister to the lost in hopes that none should perish. 2 Peter 3:9 says, "The Lord is not slack concerning his promise, as some men count slackness; but is longsuffering to us-ward, not willing that any should perish, but that all should come to repentance.

Taking an active role in missions is a sacrifice because not many people are signing up these days to do the work of missions or missionaries. In America the decline of missionaries being sent out or going overseas is steadily *decreasing*. The central task of evangelism within the 10/40 window of the world. Whereas, missionaries haven't even begun to reach out and evangelize in these areas amongst these people groups, this ought not be the church should be advancing to these regions for the sake of the gospel and for the advancement of the Kingdom of God.

The lifestyle of missionaries in these remote areas is often faced with hostility and yet many of them are addicted to getting the gospel out to the point that they sacrifice their lives. Many have died while spreading the gospel and many have remained alive and faithful however, still not enough of the gospel is being propagated in theses restricted nations. Being prepared to go where God wants and tells you to go is a huge sacrifice for a missionary. Jesus Himself and the disciple that worked with Him on his missionary journeys had to give up and sacrifice a lot to walk and work with Jesus. Matter of fact Jesus said:

- "Whoever wants to be my disciple must deny themselves and take up their cross and follow me "(Matthew 16:24).

- "Come, follow me," Jesus said, "and I will send you out to fish for people" (Mark 1:16-18).
- "With man this is impossible, but not with God; all things are possible with God." Then Peter spoke up, "We have left everything to follow you!" "Truly I tell you," Jesus replied, "no one who has left home or brothers or sisters or mother or father or children or fields for me and the gospel" (Mark 10:27-29).
- "You still lack one thing. Sell everything you have and give to the poor, and you will have treasure in heaven. Then come, follow me" (Luke 18:21-23).

The greatest question a missionary must ask themselves is, "I'm I willing to die for the gospel's sake?" With all the persecution and reject that comes along with the life of a missionary. The rewards of seeing someone that was destined to a burning hell come to the Lord Jesus Christ outweighs all the persecution in the world. The missionary must be prepared both mentally and physically to do the work of missionary and an evangelist for the places that God may be sending them to. Being a martyr for Christ isn't a bad thing. However, more times than most God's will, is to always make a way of escape when danger is present.

All throughout Apostle Paul's ministry he made many missionary journeys. God was always with him to sustain him and to protect him. There came a time when the Apostle said it himself. "I have fought a good fight, I have finished my course, I have kept the faith" (2 Timothy 4:6-8). We will all die one day and once course of life is finished what better way to die than doing the will of God. Winning souls and nations for Jesus is an awesome testimony and reward to kingdom of God and for the Lord Jesus Christ.

Journal Notes for Soul Winning Tactics:

_____

_____

_____

_____

_____

_____

_____

_____

IX

Effects of Prayer and the Rewards of Soul Winning

Prayer is one of the most effective ways to prepare for the harvest and the effectual prayers of the righteous avails much (James 5:16). Prayer is not so much for the actual harvest as it is for the labors. When going out to witness at evangelistic outings, events, and during one-on one evangelism prayer is what prepares the way for the harvest. Note, Jesus never said pray for souls however, He did say pray to the Lord of the harvest that He would send forth labors into the world (Luke).

Prayer prepares the reaper and the harvest field for the increase of souls to be saved. Prayer is a strategic weapon that can be used to stay the hand of the enemy and to soften the hearts of men both reapers (labors) and the people you're sent to minister reconciliation to. We are to pray for all people and all nations because God's will be, that all men be saved and to come into the saving revelation knowledge of which He is (the truth).

Always pray accordingly to the word of God that the Lord of the harvest would send forth laborers (Matt. 9:36-38). Pray for boldness and clarity in sharing the Gospel (Eph. 6:18-20; Col. 4:4). Pray that doors would open to ministry reconciliation, the kingdom of God, so that the gospel can be preached without hindrance (Rom. 15:30-32; Col. 4:3; 2 Thess. 3:1-2). Pray God's protection would be upon the labors and missionaries as they spread the message of the Gospel (2 Thess. 3:1-3. In addition, pray before connecting people with God, and continue to connect with God about people throughout the whole process. Why pray all this? Because:

- God made us a royal priesthood, so it is our priestly duty. (1 Peter 2:5,9; Rev. 1:6)
- God set the Biblical models, so we should do likewise. (Gen. 18:23-32 - Abraham; Ex. 32:7-14, 31-32 - Moses; I Kings 18:36-37 - Elijah; and others, including Jesus)
- God's desire is for people to be saved so we pray for His will to be done. (Ezek. 33:11; Luke. 19:10; 1 Tim. 2:3-4; 2 Pet. 3:9; Matt. 6:10)
- God has an enemy, Satan, who does not want God's will to be done on the earth, so we must submit ourselves to God and stand in His power and authority over the enemy. (Luke. 8:11-12; Jn. 12:31-32; 14:30; 16:11; Eph. 6:10-18; James 4:7-10; Rev. 12:9)

- God looks for people to stand in the gap and so be available to Him. (Ps. 106:23; Isa. 59:16; Ezek. 22:30-31)
- God works through prayer, so it only makes sense for prayer to be an integral part of any outreach or evangelism effort. (James 5:16-18)

Likewise, prayer is essential in the Christian's life. Without it your witness will be far less effective, and you will be far more vulnerable to the enemy. When you witness, you need the blessing and support of the Lord. You need to be in fellowship with Him. Prayer makes this all possible.

When you witness you plant the seeds of the Gospel, but it is God who gives the increase (1 Cor. 3:6-7). In prayer we ask God to give growth. In prayer you ask God to convict the unrepentant of their sin and by that awaken in them the need for salvation. In prayer you, "...let your requests be made known to God," (Phil. 4:6). Think back to your own conversion. Were there people praying and requesting your salvation?

Jesus prayed frequently (Matt. 14:23; 26:36; Mark 6:46; Luke 5:16; John 17). Paul prayed (Rom. 1:9; Eph. 1:16). Stephen prayed (Acts 7:55-60). You must pray. God wants you to pray to Him and have fellowship with Him (John 1:1-4). Why? One reason is that our battle is not against flesh and blood but against powers and the spiritual forces of darkness (Eph. 6:12). That is where the real battle is, in the spiritual realm. You need prayer. Prayer is one of God's ordained means for you to do spiritual warfare, and sharing the Gospel is spiritual warfare.

Another reason to pray is so you can influence God with your prayers. Pray for more people to witness. Jesus specifically asked you to pray to the Father and ask Him to send workers into the field (Matt. 9:37-38). What is the field? It is the world of sinners. Who are the workers? They are people like you. Jesus wants people to find salvation and enjoy eternal fellowship with Him. He wants you to preach the Gospel. He has given the command "go therefore and make disciples of all the nations..." (Matt. 28:19). Your witness for God may or may not be verbal. But either way, you need to pray and ask God to give you strength, love, and insight.

Pray for compassion for the lost. Compassion is a necessary element in witnessing. It motivates you to speak, to teach, and to pray for others to come into the kingdom of God. Compassion helps you to cry over the lost and to come to God in humble request for their salvation. Paul said, "Brethren, my heart's desire and my prayer to God for them is for their salvation," (Rom. 10:1). Pray for the desire to witness. Pray this regularly and watch the Lord change you and give you a desire to reach out and tell people about Jesus. God will grant your prayers and joy will fill your heart as you fulfill the command of God by witnessing.

Pray for boldness. Pray for the courage to step out in faith and speak up when needed. Many Christians are timid because speaking a word for the sake of the Lord can be risky and frightening. Boldness gives you the courage to risk ridicule and to endure the scorn. Ask God for it. "For God has not given us a spirit of timidity, but of power and love and discipline. Therefore, do not be ashamed of the testimony of our Lord," (2 Tim. 1:7-8).

Pray to the Lord to bind Satan and his angels. There is a hierarchy of demons seeking to hinder your witness and steal the seeds of the Gospel that you plant. You cannot fight spirits with reason or flesh and blood, but you can ask the Lord to fight. With prayer you can assault the camp of the enemy and weaken his false kingdom. Prayer is a mighty tool, a powerful tool. You need it if you are going to witness.

Prayer is important for many reasons, especially for witnessing. But prayer can be hindered. So that your prayers and witnessing might be as effective as possible, a discussion of the hindrances of prayer is necessary. Do any of the following apply to you? Sin hinders prayer. "If I regard wickedness in my heart, the Lord will not hear," (Psalm 66:18). We all sin, but do you have unconfessed and un-repented sin in your life? If so, confess your sin, repent from it as you are commanded in Acts 17:30, and continue in witnessing and prayer.

Doubt hinders prayer. "But let him ask in faith without any doubting, for the one who doubts is like the surf of the sea driven and tossed by the wind," (James 1:6). We all doubt. We all fail. But when you doubt be reminded of the man who said to Jesus, "Lord I believe, help my unbelief" (Mark 9:24). He believed and yet doubted, and Jesus granted his request. Remember that God has given a measure of faith to every man (Rom. 12:3). Trust God, even when you have doubts. It does not matter necessarily how much faith you have as much as whom your faith is in. Put what faith you have in Jesus. Trust Him. Watch Him be faithful to you.

Pride hinders prayer. Jesus spoke of the Pharisee and the tax-gatherer who both were praying. The Pharisee boasted about himself while the tax-gatherer asked for mercy from God. Jesus said in Luke 18:14 regarding the tax-gatherer, "I tell you; this man went down to his house justified rather than the other." Jesus shows us that pride is sin and that it hinders prayer (James 4:6). Have the same attitude that Jesus had in heaven in His full glory as He had on Earth as a man. He was humble. If you are prideful, confess it as sin, repent, and continue in humility.

Poor relationships with God and people can hinder prayers. This may seem a little out of place here, but it isn't. A proper relationship with your spouse is very important. If there are problems because of selfishness, pride, argument, anger, un-forgiveness, or any of the other obstacles that can develop in marriage, then your prayers will be hindered. How are you doing with your mate? Are you witnessing while there is anger between you two?

In Matt. 5:23-24 Jesus said, "If therefore you are presenting your offering at the altar, and there remember that your brother has something against you, leave your offering there before the altar, and go your way; first be reconciled to your brother, and then come and present your offering." Are you reconciled to your wife or husband (for that matter, anyone you know with whom there is strife) before you offer sacrifices of witnessing and prayer to the Lord? If not, then be reconciled, so your prayers won't be hindered. 1

Pet. 3:7 says, "You husbands likewise, live with your wives in an understanding way, as with a weaker vessel, since she is a woman; and grant her honor as a fellow heir of the grace of life, so that your prayers may not be hindered."

Evangelism is not an event nor is it something we just do as a part of a type of church program or event. Evangelism is a lifestyle. There are rewards in witnessing. The bible says he that wins souls is wise (Proverbs 11:30). Therefore, one of the rewards that come with being an effective witness is the believer gains wisdom. Wisdom is a very rewarding and every believer needs wisdom to be able to function and to be successful in life.

Church growth in the 21st Century church is one of the major rewards to soul winning. However, the church needs a revival marked by the Acts of the Holy Spirit with signs and wonders following. So many are asleep and comatose, so to speak and the only thing that's going to awaken the church in this hour is a quickening and a fresh out pouring of the Holy Spirit within the earth to awaken, make alive again, men, women, boys and girls to the things of God.

In addition, because of a revival many will be released into their calling and many ministries will be birthed because of a true revival. As noted earlier with the Azusa Street revival, many missionaries and churches were birthed and sent out because of the revival. Another lesson learned from studying the revival is that unity amongst the brethren is always heightened and a true sign that revival has come. Denominational barriers are broken, and racial reconciliation is also attributed to a true revival.

In this season and times when people are more susceptible and open to hear and receive the gospel of the Lord Jesus Christ. The church must strive to preach the gospel, where Christ has not already been named or mentioned, lest we should build upon another man's foundation. For, as it is written, to them whom Jesus was not spoken of, that they shall see: and to them that have not heard that they shall hear. For we are sent to win the lost at all cost and not just to those that have already heard (Romans 15:19-21).

God loves people and every minute someone dies without knowing Jesus Christ as their Lord and Savior. If the church doesn't go and tell people of God's saving grace, then who will? Share the love of Christ today with someone and be a witness to them before it's too late! Through mighty signs and wonders and by the power of the Holy Spirit, we must preach the gospel of Christ.

BIBLIOGROPHY

Dake, F. (2010). 5th ed. *Dake's annotated reference bible: Old and New Testament.* Lawrence, GA. Dake Publishing, Inc.

Easterling, J. C. (2007). David Yonggi Cho and the growth of the Yoido Full Gospel Church *Mission-ology*, 35 (2), 254-255. Retrieved October 5, 2011, from ATLA Religion Database. *English Dictionary - Complete & Unabridged 10th Edition.* Retrieved October 07, 2011, from Dictionary.com website:
http://dictionary.reference.com/browse/evangelist

Global Christianity (2011) *A Report on the Size and Distribution of the World's Christian Population.* Retrieved March 18, 2012 from Analysis http://www.pewforum.org/Christian/Global-Christianity-exec.aspx

Halley, H. (1962). *Halley's Bible Handbook.* Zondervan Publishing House, Grand Rapids, MI.

Horton, D. (Ed.). (2006) *The portable seminary: A master's level overview in one volume.* Grand Rapids, MI: Bethany House Publishers.

Lockyer, H. (1986). *Nelson's Illustrated Bible Dictionary*. New York, New York: Thomas Nelson Publishers.

Tapia, A. (1993). New look for missionaries: third world finds that the west is ripe for the harvest. *Christianity Today*, 37 (1104, 64. Retrieved October 5, 2011, from Academic Research Premier Database.

Shibley, D. (2001). *The mission addiction: Capturing God's passion for the world.* Lake   Mary, FL: Charisma House. Sermon index (2012). Retrieved April 10, 2012, from http://www.sermonindex.net/modules/newbb/viewtopic.php?topic_id=34725&forum=35&2 Inspiring quotes to live by (2012). Retrieved April 10, 2012 from http://www.soulwinning.info/gs/quotes.htm

Appendix A

Salvation Scriptures in its Simplest Form

This section will help with memorizing pertinent scriptures that are essential to leading a person to Christ. Tag your bibles with sticky notes and memorize the scriptures so you will know them and be able to quote them. People will ask you questions, and you can't be afraid to answer their questions with the word of God.

The Need:

Romans 5:12 (read and show people their need for salvation)
"Wherefore, as by one-man sin entered into the world, and death by sin; and so, death passed upon all men, for that all have sinned."
Because of Adams sin, sin passed upon all men. Therefore, all mankind needs to be reconciled back to God through Jesus.

The Solution:

St. John 3:16 (read and show people God's solution for their sins)
"For God so loved the world that he gave his only begotten Son, that whosoever believeth in him should not perish, but have everlasting life."
God's solution to mankind sin was to send Jesus into to the earth to die in man's stead, and to redeem mankind back to Him-self. Jesus took the sins of the world

upon himself and if any man believeth on him he shall have everlasting life in heaven once he departs this earth.

The Name of the Solution:

Acts 4:12 (read and show people the name that they must be saved by and in). Neither is there salvation in any other: for there is none other name under heaven given among men, whereby we must be saved.

How to Apply the Solution:

Romans 10: 8,9,10 and 13 (read and show people how to receive Jesus as their personal Lord and Savior). But what saith it? The word is nigh thee, even in thy mouth, and in thy heart: that is, the word of faith, which we preach; That if thou shall confess with thy mouth the Lord Jesus and shall believe in thine heart that God hath raised him from the dead, thou shall be saved. For with the heart man believeth unto righteousness; and with the mouth confession is made unto salvation. For whosoever shall call upon the name of the Lord shall be saved.

The Gift:

Ephesians 2: 8-9 (read and show people that Jesus is a gift to salvation and not their works). For by grace are ye saved through faith; and that not of yourselves: it is the gift of God not of works, lest any man should boast

The Right to receive this Gift:

John 1:12 (read and show people that they have a right to receive salvation)
But as many as received him, to them gave, He power to become the sons of God, even to them that believe on his name.

God so loved the world that he sent His only begotten

Son to save the world from their sins!

John 3:16

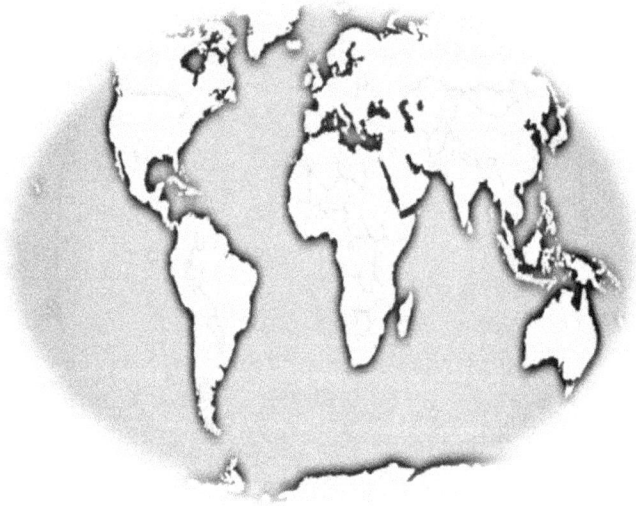

Appendix B

The Sinner's Prayer

The sinner's prayer is an example of how to pray with someone the prayer of faith, to receive Jesus Christ as their personal Lord and Savior. Always pray this prayer out loud and have the person you are witnessing to, too pray and repeat it out loud with you as well.

The Prayer for the Lost

Have those you minister salvation to repeat after you this prayer...

I believe in my heart that Jesus Christ is the Son of God. I believe He died for me, was buried and rose from the grave bearing all my sins for me. Therefore, I take Him as my Savior. Dear Jesus, come into my heart now. I believe in my heart and I confess with my mouth that you are Lord. I repent of my sins and make you my personal Lord and Savior this day and forever more. Therefore, I am born again. (See Romans 10: 8, 9, 10, 13).

Therefore, being **justified by faith**, we have peace with God through our Lord Jesus Christ: By whom also we have access by faith into this grace.

Romans 5: 1-5

Appendix C

Street Ministry and Evangelism Techniques

There are many techniques and methods that one can use to minister reconciliation to a lost soul. However, God has outlined some specific methodologies in His word that will help believers to be an effective witness. Jesus was the greatest evangelist of His day and time and He also taught His disciples how to be effective witnesses. Remember Jesus' encounter with the woman at the well? This one woman changed a whole community after just one encounter with Jesus and she too became a great evangelist and witness for the Lord Jesus Christ and the Kingdom of God.

Times and Locations

- ❖ There should always be a set time in which team members meet to go out to witness, and a return time.
- ❖ In addition, a pre-determined location for all meetings must be determined.
- ❖ Leadership should get before God before the day of going out to get guidance and directions to which location team members are to be dispatched.
- ❖ Always follow Holy Spirits guidance. For the scripture says in John 16:13, "Howbeit when he, the Spirit of truth, is come, he will guide you into all truth: for he shall not speak of himself; but whatsoever he shall hear, that shall he speak:
- ❖ And he will show you things to come. Holy Spirit knows the exact location to where the harvest of people that need salvation is and He also knows whose heart is open and ready to receive.

Prayer and Soul Winning

It's imperative that corporate prayer be established before going out to witness. Corporate prayer should be done prior to departure and day of soul winning (street witnessing, door to door, etc.) pray for at least 30 minutes and bring a word. Bind the enemy, bind fear, and loose angels. **Note: every failure is a prayer failure.**

Street Witnessing Confessions

Confessions are a great way for everyone to get into agreement with the purpose of evangelizing. Confessions also help team members get excited about soul winning and releases fear of witnessing.

Team Members

Teams are to be sent out in pairs. One prays while the other minister's salvation.

Street Witnessing Materials

1. Bibles
2. Gospel Tracts
3. Ink Pens
4. Demographic Forms (use for ministry follow-ups and outreach records)
Information literature for new convert to take with them (containing the steps they will need to follow now that they have received salvation). Literature on how they can live and walk in the new birth and life of Jesus Christ.

Listed below are the six essential things that must be included in literature. After new converts receive Jesus Christ into their hearts they need to:

1. Get involved in a local church, to be discipled so they can grow in God.
2. Read the Bible daily.
3. Pray to God daily and communicate with Him like He's a friend.
4. Get water baptized.
5. Live a pure and holy lifestyle before God.
6. Share with others what has happened and what Jesus has done for them.

Dress Code

Ministry uniforms if necessary. Some ministries use color codes to wear while out on the streets or while doing missions, so they can be distinguished and recognized by other team members. It is always wise to not over dress or under dress. Always dress appropriate to the weather and culture when witnessing and evangelizing. However, a dress code may not be necessary if what the team is wearing does not *distract* the people they are witnessing to; away from the word of God.

Note: Always dress appropriate to the culture and community that you are witnessing in. And always be mindful that your outer appearance is what people notice first.

Appendix D

Ministry Resources

Order Bibles through Biblical, which is part of the merger between International Bible Society and Send the Light. For 200 years International Bible Society (IBS) shared God's Word around the world. Through two centuries of ministry, IBS provided Scriptures to soldiers on battlefields, inmates in prisons, immigrants, the poor, and anyone who needs the hope of the Bible. Visit them online to order Bibles in bulk at http://www.biblicadirect.com

The American Bible Society has made the Bible available to every person in a language and format they can understand and afford so all people may experience its life-changing message. To order Bibles in bulk visit http://www.bibles.com

Fellowship Tract League is an organization where you can order free gospel tracts for yourself, your ministry, and or your church: http://www.fellowshiptractleague.org/index.html

The Tract League has over 300 tract titles in stock. Tracts for unbelievers are designed to point to Jesus Christ as the only way of salvation, sharing the Gospel message. Tracts for believers encourage greater Christian faith, give comfort through hard times, or persuade believers to become more active in church. Please feel free to browse our selection of Christian tracts, or request a sample of what tracts are available at: http://tractleague.com/

Ministry Tools Resource Center is about equipping Christians for ministry. This online ministry training and resources can help, beginning with yourself and if you want to equip others, visit: http://mintools.com/

Revolution in World Missions – Do you long to let go of self-centeredness and be more eternally minded? Do you desire to make a difference in the lost world but aren't sure how to go about it? Change your life with the gripping message in Revolution in World Missions can radically change your perspective than order your free copy of the book at: http://www.gfa.org/offer/freebook

Evangelism 101 (World Outreach and Missions) Official Face Book page
This page was designed and created to inform and to equip the body of Christ on how to minister reconciliation outside the four walls, through witnessing, evangelizing, outreach, & missions. All Post & Status updates are edifying, encouraging, and empowering as you get ready to be equipped to win the lost at all cost in that wonderful name above all names... Jesus Christ the son of the living God! Follow link at: https://www.facebook.com/evangelism101/?ref=bookmarks

Glossary

Anointed - to consecrate or make sacred in a ceremony that includes the applying of oil; to dedicate to the service of God.

Apostle – a messenger chosen by God and sent forth to preach the gospel; any prominent Christian missionary; especially one who first converts a nation or people; an ardent early supporter of a cause; as one who reforms or a reformer of a movement, etc.

Believe – to have confidence or faith in; to have full assurance in the truth of (a positive assertion, story, etc.); give credence to; to have faith in the reliability, honesty, and benevolence of.

Believer - to have confidence or faith in the truth of a positive assertion; to give credence to.

Christ - the Messiah or anointed one of God as the subject of Old Testament prophecies fulfilled in throughout the New Testament. Anointed as in the Greek translation of the Hebrew word rendered "Messiah".

Christian - of, pertaining to, or derived from Jesus Christ or His teachings: a Christian faith pertaining to, believing in, or belonging to the religion based on the teachings of Jesus Christ.

Christians - exhibiting a spirit proper to a follower of Jesus Christ; Christ like; decent; a person who believes in Jesus Christ; adherent of Christianity; a person who exemplifies in his or her life the teachings of Christ.

Church – the whole body of Christian believers; any division of this body professing the same creed and acknowledging the same ecclesiastical authority; a Christian denomination; the body of Christ; individuals that believe in Jesus another name for ecclesia the called-out ones.

Calling – the act of a person or thing that calls to a vocation, profession, or trade; a summons: a strong impulse or inclination; to call, invite, summon, to imply requesting the presence or attendance of someone at a particular- place. Sending for someone, using authority or formality in making the request and (theoretically) not leaving the person free to refuse.

Cities - large or important town (in the U.S.) an incorporated municipality, usually governed by a mayor and a board of aldermen or councilmen; (in Canada) a municipality of high rank, usually based on population; a community.

Confession - An open profession of faith (Luke 12:8); an acknowledgment of sins to God (Lev. 16:21; Ezra 9:5-15; Dan. 9:3-12).

Compassion – a feeling of deep sympathy and sorrow for another who is stricken by misfortune, accompanied by a strong desire to alleviate the suffering.

Commission – an authoritative order, charge, or direction; send on a mission; a duty or task committed to a person or group to perform.

Covenant – an agreement, usually formal, between two or more persons to do or not do something specified; an incidental clause in such an agreement; Ecclesiastical, solemn agreement between the members of a church to act together in harmony with the precepts of the gospel; Bible, the conditional promises made to humanity by God, as revealed in Scripture.

Crucified – to put to death by nailing or binding the hands and feet to a cross; to treat with gross injustice; persecute; torment; torture; to subdue (passion, sin, etc.).

Deliverance – salvation; rescue from moral corruption or evil; action of setting free" in physical or spiritual senses.

Disciple - a personal follower of Jesus during his life, especially one of the twelve Apostles; A follower or student of the teaching of Jesus.

Evangelism – is spreading the gospel and proclaiming Jesus Christ as Savior to those that don't know him. Persuading people to become his disciples and to become members of His kingdom.

Evangelist - an occasional preacher, sometimes itinerant and often preaching at meeting in open air; a preacher of the Christian gospel; any zealous advocate of a cause; another word for revivalist.

Fasting - an abstinence from food or a limiting of one's food, especially when voluntary and as a consecration observance; a day or period of fasting.

Go - to move or proceed, especially to or from something: be in motion; function or perform as required.

Groups – any collection or assemblage of persons or things; cluster; aggregation: several persons or things ranged or considered together as being related in some way. Harvest – to gather or reap; to gather from the fields; to gain, win, acquire.

Heart – the center of the total personality, especially with reference to intuition, feeling, or emotion; the center of emotion, especially as contrasted to the head as the center of the intellect; capacity for sympathy; feeling; affection.

Holy Spirit – the spirit of God; the presence of God; Holy Ghost; the third person of the Trinity.

Intercession – a prayer to God on behalf of another as in pleading on behalf of another.

Lost – having gone astray or missed the way; bewildered as to place, being something that someone has failed to win.

Love – God's benevolent attitude towards man; man's attitude of reverent devotion towards God.

Minister – one who acts upon the authority of God; a servant; a member of the clergy; a person who acts as the agent or servant of another; performs the sacerdotal functions. Of the church; to give service, care, or aid; attend, as to wants or necessities of others.

Missionary – person sent by a church into an area to carry on evangelism or other activities, as educational or hospital work. A person who is sent on a mission to persuade or to convert others.

Missions - originally of Jesuits sending members abroad; "act of sending," "to send," oldest form probably of unknown origin; "body of persons sent to a foreign or peoples to preach the gospel.

Nation - a large body of people, associated with a particular territory, that is sufficiently conscious of its unity to seek or to possess a government peculiarly its own.

Outreach - to reach beyond the four walls; Exceed out into the community as in missions, ministry, and/ or street evangelism usually with for food, clothing, resources and the with the gospel of Jesus Christ.

Para- church – are Christian faith-based organizations that work outside of and across denominations lines to engage in outreach, missions, and evangelism, usually independent of church oversight. The popular definition of a para-church group is any non-church based Christian entity or ministry.

Pastor - a minister or priest in charge of a church; a clergyman or priest in charge of a congregation; a person who exercises spiritual guidance over a number of people; an Archaic word for shepherd; one who God has entrusted to lead His people.

Prayer - communion with God as an act of worship, as in supplication, thanksgiving, adoration, or confession either public or private, spent mainly or wholly petitioning.

Prophet – a person who hears directly from God and speaks for God by divine inspiration; recognized and inspired to utter special revelations and predictions.; See 1 Cor. 12:28; a seer in spiritual matters; someone who can foretell the future. Prophets often make predictions which confirm them authority when the predictions came true. However, their central mission is to change the lives of God's people.

Reapers – A person, who gathers, wins, gets, brings in or takes in the harvest.

Revival - an awakening, in a church or community; an evangelistic meeting or service intended to affect such a reawakening those present.

Revivalist - a person, especially a member of the clergy, who promotes or holds religious revivals.

Salvation - deliverance from the power and penalty of sin; redemption from the penalties ensuing from sin; reference to the great deliverance from the guilt and the pollution of sin wrought out by Jesus Christ, "the great salvation" (Heb. 2:3).

Send - to cause, permit, or enable to go; to dispatch with a designated mission.

Souls – regarded as a distinct entity separate from the body, and commonly held to be separable in existence from the body; the spiritual part of humans as distinct from the physical part; the spiritual part of humans regarded in its moral aspect, or as believed to survive death and be subject to happiness or misery in a life to come.

Teacher – one who teaches or instructs in the word of God; one who disciples others.

Teams – several or more persons associated in some joint action; to gather or join in a team, a band, or a cooperative effort.

Win – to succeed in reaching; to get by effort, as through labor; the range of influence.

Wisdom - the ability or result of an ability to think and act utilizing knowledge, experience, understanding, common sense, and insight; soundness of mind; a wise act or saying.

Witness – to bear witness of; to testify of; give or afford evidence of the gospel.

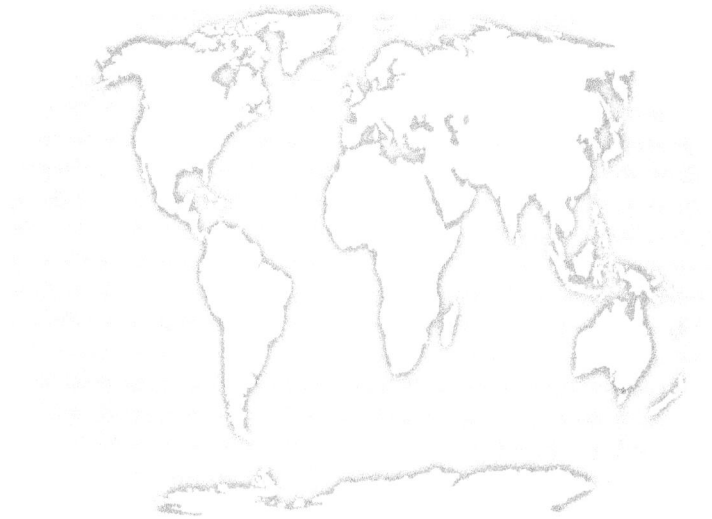

Go into all the world and preach the gospel,
to every creature!

Mark 16:15

HE WHO WINS SOULS IS WISE!

PROVERBS 11:30

Soul Winning Scriptures

Ephesians 4:11

He gave some, apostles; and some, prophets; and some, evangelists; and some, pastors and teachers.

2 Timothy 4:5

But watch thou in all things, endure afflictions, do the work of an evangelist, make full proof of thy ministry.

2 Corinthians 5:18

And all things are of God, who hath reconciled us to himself by Jesus Christ, and hath given to us the ministry of reconciliation.

2 Corinthians 5:19

To wit, that God was in Christ, reconciling the world unto himself, not imputing their trespasses unto them; and hath committed unto us the word of reconciliation.

Acts 2:41

Then they that gladly received his word were baptized: and the same day there were added unto them about three thousand souls.

Matthew 24:14

And this gospel of the kingdom shall be preached in the entire world for a witness unto all nations; and then shall the end come.

John 1:7

The same came for a witness, to bear witness of the Light that all men through him might believe.

Acts 1:8

But ye shall receive power, after that the Holy Ghost is come upon you: and ye shall be witnesses unto me both in Jerusalem, and in all Judaea, and in Samaria, and unto the uttermost part of the earth.

Acts 2:32

This Jesus hath God raised up, whereof we all are witnesses.

Acts 3:15

And killed the Prince of life, whom God hath raised from the dead; whereof we are witnesses.

Luke 1:77

To give knowledge of salvation unto his people by the remission of their sins.

Luke 15:10

Likewise, I say unto you, there is joy in the presence of the angels of God over one sinner that repent.

Acts 4:12

Neither is there salvation in any other: for there is none other name under heaven given among men, whereby we must be saved.

Romans 1:16

For I am not ashamed of the gospel of Christ: for it is the power of God unto salvation to everyone that believeth; to the Jew first, and also to the Greek.

Romans 10:10

For with the heart man believeth unto righteousness; and with the mouth confession is made unto salvation.

Romans 13:11

And that, knowing the time, that now it is high time to awake out of sleep: for now, is our salvation nearer than when we believed.

Ephesians 1:13

In whom ye also trusted, after that ye heard the word of truth, the gospel of your salvation: in whom also after that ye believed, ye were sealed with that holy Spirit of promise.

Matthew 9:37

Then saith he unto his disciples, the harvest truly is plenteous, but the laborers are few.

Matthew 9:38

Pray ye therefore the Lord of the harvest, that he will send forth laborers into his harvest.

Luke 10:2

Therefore, said he unto them, the harvest truly is great, but the laborers are few: pray ye therefore the Lord of the harvest, that he would send forth laborers into his harvest.

John 4:35

Say not there are yet four months, and then cometh harvest? Behold, I say unto you, lift up your eyes, and look on the
fields; for they are white already to harvest.

Revelation 14:15

And another angel came out of the temple, crying with a loud voice to him that sat on the cloud, thrust in thy sickle, and reap, for the time is come for thee to reap; for the harvest of the earth is ripe.

Mark 6:12

And they went out and preached that men should repent.

Mark 16:15

and he said unto them, go ye into all the world, and preach the gospel to every creature.

Mark 16:20

And they went forth, and preached everywhere, the Lord working with them, and confirming the word with signs following.

Luke 4:18

The Spirit of the Lord is upon me, because he hath anointed me to preach the gospel to the poor; he hath sent me to heal the brokenhearted, to preach deliverance to the captives, and recovering of sight to the blind, to set at liberty them that are bruised.

Acts 8:4

Therefore, they that were scattered abroad went everywhere preaching the word.

Romans 10:14

How then shall they call on him in whom they have not believed? And how shall they believe in him of whom they have not heard? And how shall they hear without a preacher?

Hebrews 1:14

Are they not all ministering spirits, sent forth to minister for them who shall be heirs of salvation.

Isaiah 61:1-3

The Spirit of the Lord GOD is upon me; because the LORD hath anointed me to preach good tidings unto the meek; he hath sent me to bind up the brokenhearted, to proclaim liberty to the captives, and the opening of the prison to them that are bound; To proclaim the acceptable year of the LORD, and the day of vengeance of our God; to comfort all that mourn; To appoint unto them that mourn in Zion, to give unto them beauty for ashes, the oil of joy for mourning, the garment of praise for the spirit of heaviness; that they might be called trees of righteousness, the planting of the Lord, that he might be glorified.

John 14:5-7

Jesus saith unto him, I am the way, the truth, and the life: no man cometh unto the Father, but by me.

Matthew 28:18-20

Go ye therefore, and teach all nations, baptizing them in the name of the Father, and of the Son, and of the Holy Ghost: Teaching them to observe all things whatsoever I have commanded you: and, lo, I am with you always, even unto the end of the world. Amen.

John 20:21

Then said Jesus to them again, Peace be unto you: as my Father hath sent me, even so send I you.

James 5:20

Let him know, that he which convert the sinner from the error of his way shall save a soul from death and shall hide a multitude of sins

Dr. Christine Renee's
Soul Winning Quotes

How would Jesus equip people to win the lost? Would He be equipping them to play the organ, usher, cook, clean, wait on the pastor? I don't think so! He would be teaching them His methodology on how to win souls into the kingdom.

We are so blessed in America we can have "church" all day long, anyway, and anywhere freely. However, we have gotten so far off the Word of God and comfortable while many Christians in other countries are being persecuted and killed for even saying they are a Christian! Something to think about!

We're not called to maintain, but to advance the kingdom of God! It's time for the body of Christ to stop being so comfortable and start wins souls for the kingdom!

No more church as usual! The Mormons and Islam are advancing their agenda while we have church as usual. When are we going to take what we have learned week after week in the pews and use it out in the market-place to advance the Kingdom of God?

Arise and wake-up old sleeping giant ... for your redemption drawth nigh! And God wants all of us to minister salvation to those that don't know Him.

You don't have to wait on Sunday morning to be saved. You can be saved today, right now! Today is your day for a miracle!

We have churches full of people who have been "saved" for decades and have never won a soul to Christ yet! Something is wrong with this picture. When the bottom-line is the great commission, not your favorite preacher, not your assembly, but soul!

Some are busy building alters and God wants to build souls! Can I get a witness?

Many have become so intellectual and political these days, and that's okay! However, I want the anointing, the anointing that destroys yokes and removes burdens; the anointing that flows with signs, wonders, and the demonstration of the power of the Holy Spirit.

There needs to be a spiritual awakening a revival in the church (the believer's life). My prayer is, Lord use me and send me. I'll go and do and say what you want me to!

There's a difference between teaching (impartation), preaching, and entertainment. If you leave the building (church meeting) and all you feel is good about yourself. But can't remember what was said, or haven't benefited from the message and there's no real change in your life. Then all you have been is entertained.

I apologize if I'm not the cute little evangelist that you'd thought I'd be, with a title only. Nor am I a part of the old boys-girl's network or doc club (clique) either.

God has anointed me to preach good tidings to the meek, He has sent me to bind up the broken heart, to proclaim liberty to the captives and to set those that are bound free (Quote from Isaiah 61:1-3).

We don't seek after miracles... We expect miracles to happen!

One miracle is worth a thousand sermons! Its proof and demonstration that Jesus' ministry is still alive in the earth!

Testimony: A dear friend who *was* a private duty nurse. He and his wife both have been *born again* for over 30 years and attend church weekly. However, one day he confessed how he's watched people die in his presence without ministering salvation to them. I told him God was going to hold him accountable for not assisting or asking them to pray the *"sinners"* prayer to receive Jesus Christ as their Lord and Savior (see Ezekiel 33:11). My friend repented and vowed that he and his wife would make it their priority to minister to the lost and win souls for the kingdom of God, at all cost. And that is exactly what they are doing.

About the Author

Dr. Christine Renee is an ordained minister with a calling and desire to help equip the body of Christ to win souls and to prepare the church for worldwide discipleship. In 2008, Dr. Christine Renee resigned from secular work to attend bible college and she also founded and incorporated, Be Blessed Ministries International.

Dr. Christine Renee has won many souls into the kingdom of God. She has also partnered with several international mission's organizations and ministries to help support and spread the good news of the gospel of the Lord Jesus Christ abroad. She hosts live stream broadcasts, prayer conference calls, seminars, revivals, and she uses her social media platforms to minister and teach the word of God.

She has an Associate and Bachelor's degree in Liberal Arts; a Master's Degree in Nonprofit Management; Doctorate Degree in Ministry. In addition, Graduate Level Certificates in Leadership. And Diploma in Biblical Studies, RHEMA Correspondence, Tulsa, Oklahoma.

Notes

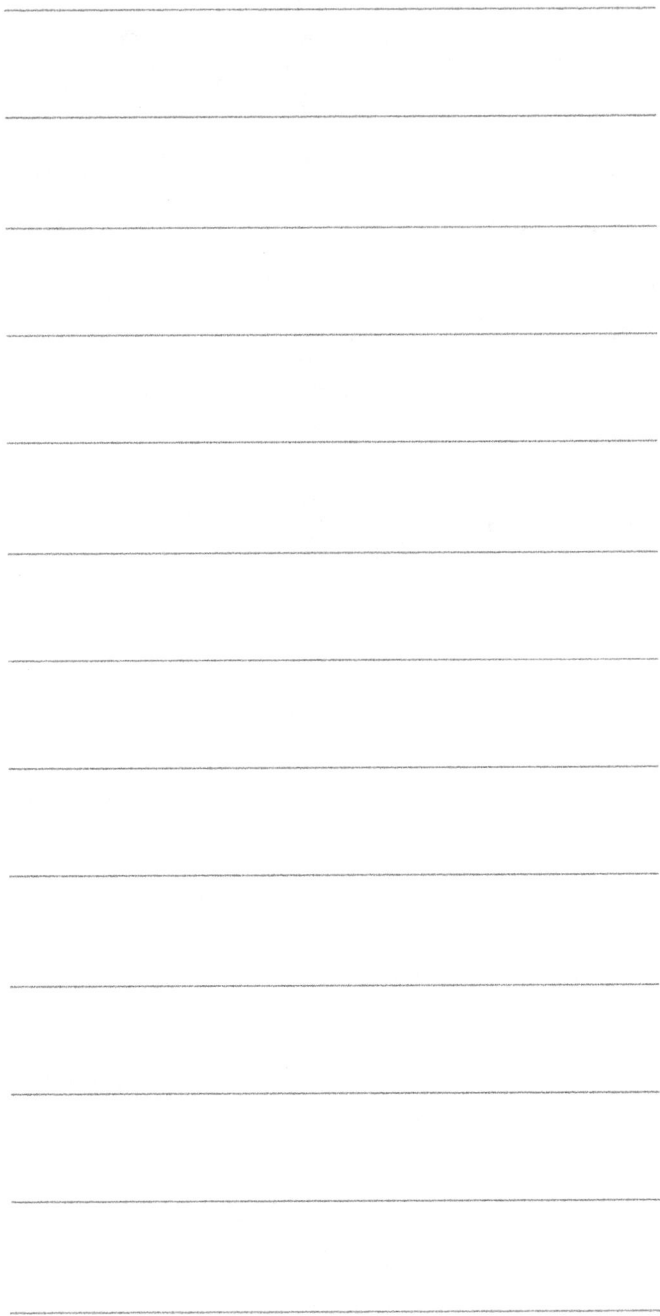

www.ingramcontent.com/pod-product-compliance
Lightning Source LLC
Chambersburg PA
CBHW021129020426
42331CB00005B/682